# Roads
# and Tracks
# of
# Britain

# Roads
# and Tracks
# of
# Britain

Christopher Taylor

**J. M. Dent & Sons Ltd**
London, Toronto and Melbourne

First published 1979
© Christopher Taylor 1979

Printed in Great Britain by
Biddles Ltd, Guildford, Surrey
and bound at the
Aldine Press, Letchworth, Herts
for J. M. Dent & Sons Ltd
Aldine House, Welbeck Street, London

Phototypeset by Trident Graphic Limited, Reigate, Surrey
This book is set in VIP Baskerville 11 on 13 point

British Library Cataloguing in Publication Data

Taylor, Christopher, b.1935
    Roads and tracks of Britain.
    1. Roads – Great Britain – History 2. Roads,
    prehistoric – Great Britain
    I. Title
    388.1'0941        HE363.G7

ISBN 0–460–04329–3

# Contents

# List of Plates

# List of Maps and Plans

# Preface

More has been written about roads and tracks than perhaps about any other aspect of the British landscape and another book on the subject might seem to be superfluous. Yet I hope that it will not be regarded as one more in the same mould. I have little interest in roads as such for one cannot date most of them, define their period of use or establish their total history. To me their real fascination lies in the way in which they affect people and the landscape and how these in turn modify the pattern of roads.

I have deliberately ignored the bulk of the literature on roads themselves and have concentrated on aspects which tell us about the whole history of the landscape. Many friends and colleagues will no doubt recognize their scholarly work on unrelated subjects, emasculated or transformed in ways they never intended or imagined. For this I apologize and beg their forgiveness.

This book is not intended as a complete history of roads. It is the result of almost twenty years in that most demanding but stimulating of occupations, adult education, where every statement is queried and discussed and where, as a result, the teacher learns more than those taught. Thus the book is an attempt to put into a coherent form those aspects of the subject which I know from experience really interested my students and over which we have argued so often.

As always, my wife has not only encouraged me but has given much practical help and advice. I am most grateful to her.

*Christopher Taylor*

# Introduction

The history of roads and trackways has for long been a subject of deep interest to anyone with the remotest curiosity about the past. Ever since modern man emerged from the intellectual ferment of the Renaissance and started to look about him for relics of the past, tracks and roads have figured prominently in his search. The first features that the earliest antiquaries examined were, naturally enough, the burial mounds and fortifications that were most clearly visible in the countryside. But any attempts to connect these monuments both in time or space soon involved such people in communications, and thus in looking for the routes by which men moved between the sites. The succeeding centuries have seen a continued growth in the study of roads of all periods and, especially in recent years, there has been a massive increase in research and a veritable flood of books and articles on various types of roads and tracks. Some of these more recent works are the result of deep and expert academic scholarship and, as a result, though of great importance to the subject, can hardly be regarded as easy reading. At the same time there have also appeared many 'popular' books on ancient trackways, most of which are largely nonsense and have little or no relevance to the truth.

The difficulties in trying to write a history of roads and tracks are manifold. One of these is that, except for certain types of Roman roads and roads deliberately engineered from the late seventeenth century onwards, most roads and tracks visible in the landscape are undated and undatable. We may see a delightful green lane wandering across the downlands of Wessex, apparently linking groups of prehistoric forts with burial mounds, or we may follow a minor road across miles of countryside from one medieval town to another, but there is no actual proof that one is a prehistoric track and the other a medieval highway. They could be of any date. Once tracks are made, even if they were produced in the first instance by wandering animals, they tend to be used by succeeding generations often for hundreds if not thousands of years. Their importance may vary across the ages: a track between two prehistoric villages might become part of a major road between towns in the Roman period, decline to a farm lane in Saxon times, be developed as a national trade route in the fourteenth century and then become an overgrown footpath by the present day. Even if we could ascertain all these changes, which is doubtful, what 'date' do we say it is?

Across the fields of my own village are two routes. One is a major A-class trunk road, one of the most overloaded in the country; the other, parallel with it, is a rough track leading towards the next village and providing a pleasant Sunday afternoon's walk. No one would perhaps think that the main road was of much historical interest, though local historians regard the track as part of the great prehistoric Icknield Way which ran across England from Wessex to East Anglia. Yet in fact though both main road and track are, very roughly speaking, on the general line of the Icknield Way, the road is much the more representative, providing as it does a long-distance route across the country. The grass-edged, rutted, stony track is in fact relatively modern and was made in 1812 when the landscape of my parish was reorganized and given a new road system. Thus the fact that it passes the site of a large Roman villa and a group of prehistoric burial mounds is of little importance; this kind of situation, which is extremely common, illustrates only too well that visible signs of apparent antiquity are not to be relied upon.

With the exception of the properly engineered Roman roads, all roads or tracks in use before the eighteenth century, and in many cases up until the early years of this century, had no proper surface. As a result they were usually deeply rutted, pot-holed and thoroughly inconvenient to use. The coming of road engineers and the improvement of means of transport from the eighteenth century onwards meant that some of the most ancient routes were transformed into modern highways with no trace of antiquity about them, while relatively recent lanes, deeply worn by only a few years of agricultural traffic, were abandoned, became grassed over and today appear as routes of high antiquity. A splendid, if somewhat unusual example of this kind can be seen on the army training ranges at Stanford in Norfolk. When the area was cleared of its inhabitants at the beginning of the Second World War, many of the old medieval lanes between the three former villages were straightened and rebuilt to take heavy military transport. As a result, none look at all medieval now. But at the same time tanks and other tracked vehicles were driven across the fields and, at certain places, produced deeply hollowed trackways. Some of these have now returned to the wild and look as fine 'ancient trackways' as it is possible to see anywhere.

On the whole roads are virtually impossible to date on the ground. The fact that they run from *A* to *B* means nothing. It may be that *A* and *B*, whether they are prehistoric circles, Roman villages or medieval cities, were placed where they are centuries before the route was established or, conversely, that the road or track was developed to or past the circle, village or city long after these were built.

Perhaps the greatest problem in the understanding of roads lies in the minds of those who wish to unravel their history. The fascination of roads and tracks, and the excitement that the process of tracing them onwards across country gives, have all too often in the past resulted in complete mental blocks and visual blindness. The same situation unfortunately still exists today. The desire to trace a line of communication, any line, to a significant point, any point, and to clothe it with romantic visions of prehistoric farmers, Roman soldiers or medieval travellers leads to greater and greater flights of fancy and in the end to total nonsense. Nowhere is this better seen than in the work of Alfred Watkins and his book of the *Old Straight Track*. The whole work has no basis in fact at all, yet most of his ideas are still widely accepted and his followers live on, combing the landscape for clues. Maps, usually the totally unsuitable small-scale variety, are examined minutely, lines are drawn across them from church to castle, from castle to hill top and hill top to stone circle, from circle to monastery and finally from monastery to a point where there is nothing at all but 'obviously there was something important there once'. Anything remotely involving an established historical fact is ignored. The evidence of scholarly work on historical documents, of scientific archaeological excavation, and worst of all, of plain common sense, is completely rejected unless it fits in with the preconceived line of argument.

The sadness about such work, quite apart from the utter futility of it all, is that it actually obscures and degrades the very real achievements of man who, from early prehistoric times right up to the present day, has shown himself to be a highly sophisticated animal, whose abilities, aims, successes and failures are nowhere better seen than in his means of communication, developed, changed and refined over the centuries. If we are really to try to understand the history of man and his roads and tracks in Britain then we must reject all the nonsense of straight tracks, ley lines and so forth and look at the evidence from history, archaeology and from the landscape with unbiased minds and without preconceived ideas. For there is much evidence easily available for us to see the truth if we desire it.

This is especially so in the case of prehistoric trackways. The recent advances in knowledge and the development of new scientific methods for the recovery of information about the ability of our remote ancestors to communicate with each other over long distances is not generally appreciated outside the specialized world of archaeologists. For most people, prehistoric man journeyed through endless primeval forests, or along high downland ridgeways guided by mounds of earth or piles of stones. The reality, as we shall see, was very different. Likewise in Roman times, the imagined picture is of straight, well-engineered roads, cutting across a primitive landscape from town to town, passing the occasional Roman villa on the way. In fact, though such roads certainly existed, they were only one part, and a very small part at that, of a complex system of routeways which covered most of the country. In the medieval period too we tend to think of roads being major routes joining the large centres of population. We forget the myriad lanes and droveways that linked village to fields, village to village and village to town. Even the relatively modern roads of Britain, that is, the turnpikes of the eighteenth and nineteenth centuries, and the enclosure roads of the same period, which together make up over 75 per cent of our present communications pattern, are little recognized or understood. Similarly roads of this century, the main arterial routes, the bypasses and the motorways, are rarely appreciated for what they do for us and our environment.

In this book we shall look at the different types of roads and trackways that have developed or that have been constructed in Britain throughout the centuries. We shall discover their possible dates, their function and their form and, probably much more important, we shall look at the effect of these routeways on man and the landscape. For roads and tracks do much more than just enable people to travel from one place to another. They affect the position and the layout of our towns, the shape of our villages and indeed a great deal of our whole environment. At the same time roads and tracks of all ages have been influnced by the land through which they pass and the demands made on them by man at different stages in his technological advance.

Finally the heritage of roads is still all about us – and not as interesting historical monuments, or pleasant walks, but as a vital part of twentieth-century life. Container lorries, bound for the continent, still use prehistoric trackways; long-distance coaches continue to hurtle along Roman roads; many farmers depend on medieval lanes to reach their land. The history of roads is not the study of the dead past but of the living present.

# 1   Prehistoric Trackways

Of all types of roads and tracks, those of the prehistoric period in Britain are perhaps the most difficult to discuss. One reason is that, as has already been said, all but a few are quite impossible to date. More important, however, is that most people have completely the wrong impression of all aspects of prehistoric society and thus of its means of communication. This impression is based on two grave misconceptions which are almost impossible to remove. The first of these is that prehistoric people were primitive and unsophisticated; the second that they were totally controlled by their environment. Neither is true. Most prehistoric people were extremely sophisticated and over the centuries learnt to dominate their environment in a way that is still largely unappreciated. Even 2000 years before the birth of Christ there was in Britain a technically advanced and commercially well-developed society with permanent settlements and agriculture, and with a complex pattern of communications all over the country based on long-distance trade routes and even specially constructed tracks.

Most, but not all, routeways which the earliest prehistoric people had were what one might call natural tracks. They were not deliberately constructed, of course, but gradually came into being in response to specific needs. These natural tracks are the first which we can infer from the evidence of archaeology, even if we cannot actually locate them on the ground. Though man and his ancestors occupied the British Isles during the long periods of temperate climate within the last million-year-long ice age, the story of tracks really begins at the end of the last glaciation, some 10,000 years ago, when the great ice sheets gradually retreated and finally withdrew from the British Isles. They left behind them a landscape torn apart. In the northern and western mountains the hills had been smoothed over and the valleys gouged deep by the movement of ice. As the ice disappeared the meltwaters spread vast quantities of boulders, gravel and silt over the landscape creating lakes, damming rivers and blocking valleys. Even in southern Britain, where the ice sheets never reached, the ground was heaved up and pulled apart by the freeze-thaw climate of the final years of the ice age. Here too valleys were filled with sludge, and river courses were changed.

As the climate improved this harsh landscape was gradually clothed with vegetation and the ice scars healed. At first only the mosses and other Arctic plants could survive, but by about 8000 BC the climate improved rapidly so that within about 500 years it was very similar to that of today and, in fact, continued to get even warmer. Within a very short time the bare countryside disappeared under pine trees which in turn were succeeded by birch, hazel and then elm. Finally an alder-lime-oak woodland emerged. The marshy areas which remained were edged by willows and filled with sedge. Grass moors appeared on the uplands. As the climate and the vegetation improved, rivers became rich in fish, the marshes filled with wild-fowl and the forests and grassland with wild cattle and deer. Some of the larger animals, particularly, were migratory in their habits and very soon developed set routes as they crossed the country, thus producing natural trackways. Some of these trackways were perhaps the result of seasonal movements to pasture land, but it has also been suggested that others were developed as herds moved between coastal areas and inland grazing in the search for necessary salt.

Certainly, from detailed examination by palaeobotanists and palaeozoologists in many places in the British Isles, large-scale animal movements in the centuries following the end of the last ice age seem well attested. It appears from the work of these people that wild cattle regularly migrated from the upland moors of southern Scotland and central Wales to the maritime grasslands of the Solway Firth and Cardigan Bay. To do this they would have certainly followed the 'best' routes through upland passes, along ridgeways and across rivers and streams at the most easily fordable places. So, though as always with tracks it is in the end unprovable, it seems very likely that many of our 'prehistoric trackways' were in the beginning prehistoric animal tracks. Certainly some of the great ridgetop routes such as the Icknield Way of East Anglia and the Pilgrims' Way of south-east England may well have come into existence as migratory animal routes about 8000 BC. If this is so it raises two interesting points about these great long-distance trackways which will recur later on in their history.

Firstly, migrating animals, though developing a trackway in a general sense, do not in fact travel in a follow-my-leader fashion but rather in an apparently disorganized straggle with the herd covering a relatively wide area. In open country especially, far from developing a narrow track, the animals create a broad zone of communication which might be two or three miles across, kept clear of encroaching vegetation as a result of continual use and grazing on the hoof. These broad zones of communication are exactly what we find later on in the prehistoric and even early medieval periods along great routeways of Britain. Only where the routes crossed major rivers by way of fords, or had to traverse difficult country through defiles or valleys, did the animals converge to produce narrow trackways. Later on human beings did exactly the same.

Secondly these long-distance tracks, though having a fairly definable overall route, also developed countless others along their length where groups of animals joined or left the main one. Thus all these natural animal movements finally produced a highly complicated system of what can only be called zones of communication, for to describe them as tracks produces a quite erroneous picture.

Just as important were the local tracks made by animals as they moved from pasture to woodland shelter or to drinking points. All over the country there must have been woodland paths or moorland tracks. Perhaps as early as 8000 BC, therefore, the British Isles were criss-crossed by innumerable trackways both local and long distance, developed purely by wild animals in their natural environment.

It was on this well-developed but constantly changing pattern of routeways that man for the first time began to make his influence felt. In the long centuries between the final retreat of the ice and a date which was probably around 5000 BC, the British Isles were occupied by small groups of hunter-fisher-gatherers. Archaeologists divide these peoples into two main types on the basis of their tools. The earlier group, who used rather large, coarse tools, are usually called Late Palaeolithic people; the later ones, who had acquired the techniques of making more sophisticated tools, are called Mesolithic people. For our purposes this division means very little, however, for the basic way of life of both groups was very similar and thus their part in the history of trackways is much the same.

All the evidence from the habitation sites of these people points to

the fact that they were constantly on the move as a result of the need
to search for food; by the very nature of their economy they would
make or use tracks. Yet, like all primitive people, their tracks must
have been indistinguishable from those made by the animals they
hunted. Even at the simplest level they would probably use the same
drinking places and thus inevitably take the same ways to water as
did the animals, while in forests and woodland they would tend to
move along the animal paths merely because it was the easiest way
to travel.

However, there was a much more important connection between
these people and the natural animal trackways than this, for while
they certainly lived by gathering nuts and berries, collecting shell-
fish, catching fish and hunting the smaller animals which lived all
around them such as wild-fowl, sea birds, wild pigs and even
hedgehogs and voles, the greater part of their diet was obtained from
wild cattle and particularly deer. In addition these larger animals
provided other materials badly needed and assiduously sought after,
such as hides and skins for protection and bones for various kinds of
tools and ornaments. As a result these people had to have a way of
life closely involved with the migratory herds and, in essence, had to
move with them across the countryside from summer pastures to
winter feeding grounds and back again.

The meticulous but bald descriptions of the habitation sites of
these people, written by the archaeologists who have found them,
often cover up this complex pattern of animal/man relationship,
particularly with regard to trackways. The apparently squalid
occupation areas which have been found along the coasts of southern
England, Wales and Scotland, set as they are among mounds of
limpet shells and other rubbish, are often regarded as the crude hiding
holes of people driven to the seaside by a lack of food in the winter.
Similarly the small areas of flint tools, high on the Pennine moors,
have also been seen as the remains of family groups eking out a
precarious living off the high hills. It is, however, far more likely that
these sites are the winter and summer homes of people following the
herds of animals on their seasonal movements across the country
and thus being provided with the necessities of life all the year
round.

This sophisticated interrelationship between early prehistoric man
and the animals he depended upon meant that, inevitably, he used
the same trackways and lines of movement. Man passed along them,

hunted on them, dug pitfalls in them to trap animals and, in the end, grew to know them intimately. Finally man may have actually started to modify them. The evidence for this is not as clear as we would like but there are suggestions that, towards the end of the Mesolithic period, some time after 6000 BC, man's relationship with the animals he hunted became much closer than that merely of pre-dator and prey. Palaeobotanists who have examined the grains of pollen recovered from ancient peat bogs and deeply buried soils dat-ing from this period, as well as soil specialists looking at similar deposits, have detected traces of what appear to be deliberately fired woodland areas; that is, Mesolithic people were setting fire to the forests surrounding their dwellings. Evidence for such burning has been discovered in many places including Salisbury Plain, Wytch-wood Forest in Oxfordshire and on the North Yorkshire Moors. As far as we can see this burning was part of a deliberate policy to better the grazing for the wild animals on the phosphorus-rich land thus produced, and so increase the population of the herd. Modern studies of deer in North America have shown that this can be done although, to create a long-term effect, the firing has to be repeated every few years. To judge by the large amount of evidence for Mesolithic fires at this time these people were carrying out this pro-cess successfully.

However, increasing animal numbers, concentrating them in suit-able areas and improving their quality was not enough. The single hunter or even a small group could not always depend on these fac-tors alone to produce a constant supply of food, especially during the hard winter months. The only solution was in group co-operation involving not solitary stalking and killing but group 'drives' whereby organized units of hunters followed, or, more likely, drove herds to natural or artificially created pastures where they could be killed at will. Such social groups would also tend to protect the herds they organized and schemes could have been developed to defend these herds against animal as well as other human predators.

This close relationship between man and animals, which probably evolved around 6000 BC, is important for a number of reasons. The social changes wrought in man himself in terms of co-operation with his fellows, for example, were to have great influence in later cen-turies. But how did this behaviour affect the history of trackways, which is our concern here? There are two factors to consider. The first is a general one, that the continued use of fire, combined with the more gradual overall effect of climatic alterations, began to change the face of the countryside completely and man began to control his environment. The overall forest cover was broken up and areas of downland, heath and moorland increased. The greater extent of moorland available meant that man and his animals, crossing with comparative ease, could develop more complex track systems. Of greater interest perhaps is that with increasing human control of the wild herds of animals, a new pattern of semi-natural trackways evolved, related to and integrated with the older purely natural tracks, but produced as the herds were persuaded or forced to use the new fire-created pastures or protected areas, away from their natural migration routes.

In addition to these animal trackways, whether we consider them natural or artificial, man himself began to use and develop trackways for purposes other than hunting or controlling animals. For as well as the basic need for food, which involved the following and guiding of herds of animals, there were other requirements which forced these early prehistoric people to travel. In simple terms, man started trading for certain requirements which were not easily to hand along his normal nomadic paths and this led eventually to the growth of lines of communication along which goods were passed.

Exactly how this trade was carried out, and what it consisted of, is difficult to ascertain: evidence for such activities is very hard to find by normal archaeological means. We shall probably never know whether there were individual merchants moving around the countryside selling or bartering goods to groups of migratory hunters, or whether the goods were passed on from group to group as contact was made between them. Nor can we know just how great a variety of goods was traded. We may guess that certain essentials moved about. Salt, for example, which is a basic requirement of life, was almost certainly traded in some form, but it is obvious that this commodity, perhaps more than anything else, is impossible to detect in an archaeological excavation of a site 8000 years old. Even so we do have certain clues as to what was bartered or traded in these centuries, and one good example can be seen in the tools of some groups of these people. Though flint occurs widely in southern England, many Mesolithic people, for reasons that are quite unknown to us, preferred to have tools made out of chert – a fairly pure silicaceous rock which fractures easily and can be shaped into small tools. In southern England the only place where it is found naturally is on and around the Isle of Portland, in Dorset, where it occurs both exposed in the cliffs as blocks or nodules, and as pebbles on the beaches. As one would expect, the Mesolithic people who lived in south Dorset used this chert almost exclusively for their tools – but the same material has also been found on the occupation sites of similar people further afield. Chert tools occur in Devon, Cornwall as far west as the Land's End peninsula, in Somerset, Hampshire, the Isle of Wight and in Sussex (Fig. 1). They have also been found at three places in Surrey as well as in Wiltshire and as far north as south Gloucestershire. It is very difficult to see from the available evidence which routes were used to transport this chert from Portland. Some may have been taken along the coast, perhaps by water, but in other cases overland trade can be the only answer. Certainly the finds from east Devon suggest that trade routes existed along the valleys of the River Exe and its tributaries, while the Wiltshire material indicates routeways along the River Avon. On the other hand the chert tools from Surrey suggest that the ridgeway route along the North Downs, later to become known as the Pilgrims' Way, was a possible line taken by the 'chert traders'.

On a much more localized scale there is similar evidence for complex movements of people searching for suitable materials for tools

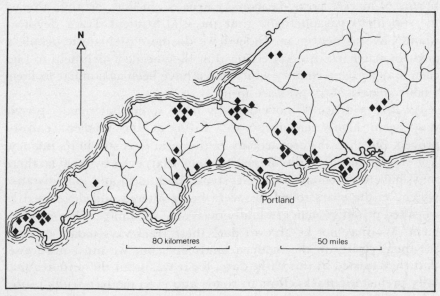

Fig. 1 Distribution of Mesolithic artefacts made from Portland chert

on the east coast of Scotland. At Morton in Fife there is a low sandy
promontory near the sea, where a Mesolithic settlement site, dated to
around 5400 BC, has been excavated (Fig. 2). The many hundreds of
stone tools and other artefacts that were found have been examined,
with the result that no less than twenty-two different kinds of stone
employed in their manufacture have been recognized. Many of the
implements were made out of types of flint which were obtained in
the general locality of the site, but others come from at least fifteen
miles away to the south. In addition a number of minerals including
chalcedony, common opal and various types of quartz, none of
which can be found in the immediate area, were being used for tools;
these can only have come from the ancient rocks of the Ochil Hills
and the Sidlaw Hills and their nearest point to the site is twenty
miles away. Other rocks found included fireclay and limestone,
which were probably obtained from areas far to the south. These
finds, somewhat uninteresting in themselves, show clearly the mobility of what was, after all, probably no more than a single family
group, for they indicate the ability of these people to cross major
rivers, including the Tay, and locate desirable sources of stone. The
dull fragments of tools also reflect their highly developed knowledge
of the topography of a wide area. They certainly do not suggest that
these people needed to find their way about the countryside by
means of marker posts, beacons, cairns, sight-lines or any other of
the ridiculous paraphernalia that the Old Straight Track devotees
would have us believe in. Indeed we do these prehistoric people a
great injustice in even conceiving that they needed such help to find
their way across a country which must have been as familiar to them
as our villages and towns are to us.

All this evidence of movement by these somewhat remote people
may seem highly unsatisfactory. Little at the moment can be
proved, but then the archaeology of these times is still in its infancy.
Yet enough has been discovered to show that, even by 4000 BC there
must have been complex track systems, both local and long distance
which, as the years rolled by, were being altered and developed as
so-called primitive man gradually overcame the limits of his environment. We may not be able to date these trackways today, or even
see them clearly in the modern landscape, but we must not forget
that they existed at this early date, for it was from these routes that
later prehistoric tracks, Roman roads and even modern trunk routes
developed.

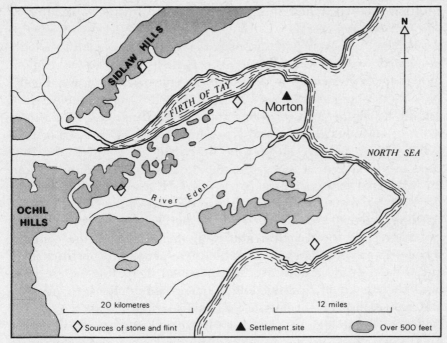

Fig. 2 Mesolithic settlement, Fife, Scotland: sources of materials for artefacts

Around 4000 BC a remarkable change took place in the history of man in Britain. The exact significance is still not clear, and many details are lacking, but the general outlines are known. New people with radically new ideas and an advanced and sophisticated technology appear for the first time, and in the succeeding centuries these people not only occupied most of the country, but also gradually passed on their way of life to the earlier Mesolithic people who lived alongside them. In some ways these Neolithic people, as they are known, were similar to the Mesolithic folk in that they also hunted the now shrinking herds of wild animals, fished and gathered. But they also had acquired the ability to make pottery and had much more advanced types of tools. From our point of view the pottery is less important than the tools, which included fine stone and flint axes capable, when aided by fire, of clearing huge areas of forest relatively easily and quickly. Perhaps even more significant was that these Neolithic people had learnt how to domesticate animals and had their own flocks of sheep and herds of cattle. In addition they knew how to grow crops and cultivated a number of different types of cereal.

Evidence of just what a complex society the Neolithic people developed can be seen all over the British Isles. Their religion, though quite mysterious to us, led to the construction of monuments such as Avebury in Wiltshire as well as many more similar sites, usually called 'henges', including those at Durrington Walls, also in Wiltshire, Mount Pleasant and Knowlton in Dorset, and Arbor Low in Derbyshire. These can only be described as 'temples' and they need to be looked at alongside the thousands of chambered and unchambered tombs or long barrows which are found all over the British Isles. Some of these sites are in the care of the Department of the Environment and are open to the public: the interested visitor can appreciate the technical ability of their builders, the complex social organization that could enable these people to construct them and wonder at mysterious rituals carried out there, but the everyday non-religious life of Neolithic folk is much more difficult to visualize and only skilled archaeologists and other scientists can recover the evidence. Yet though we cannot easily see it we must not ignore it, for it casts these people in a very different light and helps us to understand the complexities of their trackways.

Archaeologists, together with their colleagues in such sciences as palaeobotany and physics, have in the last few years radically changed our ideas on the everyday life of this period. They have shown that soon after 4000 BC extensive areas of forest were being cleared and replaced by broad open pastures and fields not confined to the traditional light chalk and limestone soils of Wessex, east Yorkshire and the Cotswolds, as is taught to every school child – but everywhere: on the barren heaths of Norfolk, in the deep valleys of Cumbria, on the lower slopes of the Welsh mountains and as far north as the Spey valley in north-eastern Scotland. Even the marks of ploughs, cut into the underlying soils as they were dragged across fields, have been found in Wiltshire. The settlements of these people have also been discovered and excavated, showing a wide variety of forms. Perhaps the most famous is at Skara Brae, in the Orkneys, where superb stone houses were found (this site has survived so well because only stone was available to the builders in those windswept islands). Elsewhere, for the most part, only wood was used to build houses, which have not survived for us to see: the traces of these Neolithic people's homes have to be carefully unearthed, using highly skilled techniques, but the results are of great interest. On Broome Heath in south Norfolk, for example, a large area of occupation, almost certainly originally a number of wooden huts, was discovered lying inside a large curving bank and ditch, which seemed to be protecting them. A similar but larger defensive enclosure has been discovered near Luton in Bedfordshire, while at Carn Brae, in Cornwall, a massive stone wall seems to have protected a group of houses. Elsewhere pits which, because they were used for storing grain, show the only recoverable trace of Neolithic farmsteads, have been found. These occur all over southern England, the south-east Midlands, East Anglia and east Yorkshire as well as in the far north of Scotland. Even where we have not, as yet, found the actual houses of these Neolithic people, we can infer where they must be from the location of the tombs of their dead. All along the western coast of Scotland and on the islands, for example, chambered tombs of this period occur widely. Many are set overlooking small fertile bays or in rich valleys which must have been the farmland of their builders.

This description of the way of life in the Neolithic period may seem a far cry from the history of its tracks, but it is important to understand what kind of society existed at this time in order to appreciate its trackways. For all the foregoing discussion about forest clearance, fields, crops and complex settlements means one thing: settled life instead of nomadism. And settled life, especially with fields and domesticated animals, means that permanent tracks are needed leading from farmstead to field, from field to pasture and from habitation to habitation. In the centuries between 4000 and 2000 BC the British Isles was becoming a well-organized and well-populated country, with great tracts of land, whether upland or lowland, managed by farmers. These facts cannot be stressed too much, for many people in the past have imagined a totally hostile, wild, marshy or forested environment, in which people eked out a primitive existence.

However, having said that there were tracks all over the country, closely integrated with the farming economy of the time, it is still very difficult to prove their existence completely to the continuing unbeliever for inevitably, except in a few special places, these tracks have not been found by archaeologists up to now. Indeed it is difficult to see how they can be found and, even if they were, how they could be dated. As has been stressed already, once a track develops it is often used by succeeding generations and thus it is impossible to recognize its beginnings, and, by and large, as the trackway consists merely of a worn line of land constantly used and thus constantly altered, the modern archaeologist is unlikely to find anything that dates it even if he does excavate it. This is the problem which faces us when we try to find Neolithic trackways. It is more than possible that many of our country lanes or even main roads occupy in part or entirely Neolithic trackways, but to prove it is beyond our capacity.

On the other hand, the picture is not entirely blank for, on rare occasions, superb trackways of this period have been found and dated, mainly because of two important factors. Firstly, the Neolithic farmers sometimes had to construct tracks across marshy ground and, secondly, this marshy ground has not only preserved these made tracks for us to find, but also contains in its make-up the materials which enable us to date them. The most remarkable of these Neolithic trackways are those which have been found in the Somerset Levels, and especially in the area between the Polden Hills and the Wedmore Ridge (Fig. 3). Here the land is not, and never has been, entirely peat marsh, and contains numerous 'islands' either of

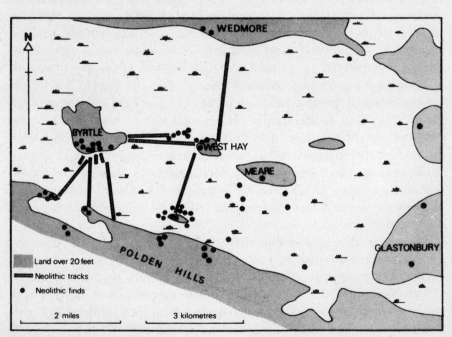

Fig. 3 Neolithic tracks and finds, Somerset Levels

hard rock or sand. These, together with the dry land of the hills to the north and south, were the homes of Neolithic farmers. Partly as a result of major drainage works, but more recently because of massive digging for garden peat, the deliberately constructed trackways of the Neolithic period constantly come to light. Over forty such trackways, dated between 2000 and 3000 BC have now been found in the Somerset Levels. The earliest ones, that is those built soon after 3000 BC, were all constructed on the same principle: bundles of twigs or brushwood, usually birch, were laid across the marshy land and held in place by pegs driven into the ground on each side. Occasionally transverse timbers were placed on the wet ground, before the bundles were put in position, to give extra support. Such trackways have been found all over the Levels and often they seem to have been constantly repaired or rebuilt.

Just before 2000 BC there is evidence for more elaborate trackways, constructed by laying planks of wood or split logs, often of alder, transversely along the line of the road and again held in place with pegs driven into the ground. The pegs were attached to the planks or logs by longitudinal stringers and the whole track was thus very substantial and stable. Estimates have been made of how much timber would have been required for this kind of track: it has been worked out that a track one mile long would require about twenty miles of planks or split logs and over 80,000 pegs up to three feet long. Yet not only are there some twelve to fourteen miles of this type of trackway known but there must be many miles as yet undiscovered. This gives us some idea of the amount of woodland that had to be cleared merely to produce this timber and, indeed, the analyses of the prehistoric pollen preserved under these tracks indicate that the amount of woodland on the adjacent hills was being greatly reduced in these centuries. The pollen also shows that open pasture and arable land were being created in place of the earlier woodland. Although these Somerset trackways are the only ones closely dated and studied, others, probably of the same period, are known from other marshland areas, notably the Cambridgeshire fenland. There too the tracks seem to link the fen edges with the 'islands' within the fens.

This, then, is the admittedly sparse evidence for locally constructed trackways of Neolithic times. But in addition to these tracks, there were other, greater routeways of national and even international importance for, as with the earlier Mesolithic peoples,

Neolithic farmers also had highly developed trade routes along which came both the necessities and the luxuries of life. Again much of the trade in commodities such as salt and skins is irrecoverable by archaeology, but thanks to modern scientific techniques other goods can be identified and traced.

Perhaps most important was the trade in stone axes. The most common material used by Neolithic people for their axes, and indeed for all their other tools such as arrow heads, scrapers and knives, was flint. In addition, however, specialized axes and other tools were made from different rocks and these, apparently greatly prized at the time, were traded all over the British Isles and even beyond. Using techniques developed by geologists to identify the mineral content of rocks, archaeologists can examine these stone axes and locate, often fairly closely, the place from whence they came. As a result, various Neolithic 'axe factories' have been discovered where specialized workmen dug out the chosen rock, shaped it into tools and then carried them away all over the country to willing buyers. The actual sites of some of these factories are known, for example the one at Langdale in Cumbria, and another in north Wales at Craig Llwdd on the Lleyn Peninsula. Other general locations for axe factories have been identified in such places as the Lizard Peninsula in Cornwall, Tievbulliagh in Northern Ireland, near Nuneaton in Warwickshire, in Charnwood Forest, Leicestershire, as well as in a number of other areas (Fig. 4). The axes made in these places have been found all over Britain, giving us a very clear idea of how far the Neolithic tradesmen travelled with their goods – and these traders must have used well-known established routeways.

One specific area can be examined in some detail, to show what happened. This is East Anglia where, apart from flint, no other rock suitable for axes occurs. Just over four hundred stone tools found within the counties of Norfolk, Suffolk, Cambridgeshire and Essex have been examined; of these nearly sixty came from Cornwall, twenty from Wales, almost ninety from the Lake District, seven from Northern Ireland, forty-one from the Whin Sill in Northumberland, and sixteen from Charnwood Forest, Leicestershire. The rest were all made from rocks not found in East Anglia, but their sources have yet to be identified. The places where most of these tools were found are known, and we can therefore plot them on a map (Figs 5 and 6). Basically they show us only where Neolithic people lived, for the majority must have been left on abandoned settlement sites or with burials. They indicate that many people dwelt along the fen edges of Cambridgeshire and Norfolk, in the valleys of the Rivers Debden, Orwell, Stour and Colne in south-east Suffolk and north-east Essex, to a lesser extent in central Norfolk, and in the Norwich area. Such a distribution incidentally makes nonsense of the older ideas that primitive people lived on the high chalkland and limestone, surrounded by forest. The picture obtained from the axes alone shows how much land these farming communities had cleared and put under cultivation and pasture.

But what does the map tell us of the routeways by which these axes reached East Anglia? Clearly we must not forget a sea-borne trade. Certainly it is possible that many of the Cornish axes could have come to these coasts by sea, but even then they were taken inland by established tracks. To take one specific example, a single axe, made from the rock at Great Langdale in the Lake District, has been found near a country lane running between the villages of Edgefield and Saxthorpe in north Norfolk. It may have reached the coast by a sea-going boat, but by what route did it reach its final location? No major rivers are nearby, so it must have been carried overland. Though we shall never know for certain the route taken, it

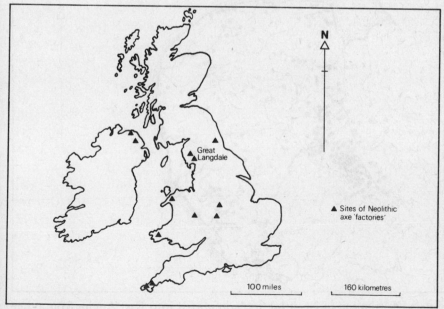

Fig. 4 Neolithic axe factories

may well be that it was carried along the same lane that exists today, wandering across the countryside, around the marshy ground, following the easy slopes. This detail is not shown on the general map (Figs. 5 and 6), but some conclusions may be drawn. The great concentration of axes along the eastern edge of the fenlands, for instance, lies alongside the line of the Icknield Way which passes to the west running north to the Wash. There can be little doubt that this was the route by which many of the axes found near it came into East Anglia. This then is evidence for the early use of one of the great prehistoric trackways of England. On the other hand the map also shows that there must have been may other tracks apart from the Icknield Way.

Yet it is worth looking at what this great trackway is today, for it is a good example of the changing use of these routeways over the centuries. The most westerly part of the Icknield Way, as it enters East Anglia at Royston in Hertfordshire, is now the A505, a major modern trunk route linking the industrial towns of Luton and Dunstable with Norwich. Just south-east of Cambridge, the Icknield Way become the A11, an even busier road joining London to Norwich

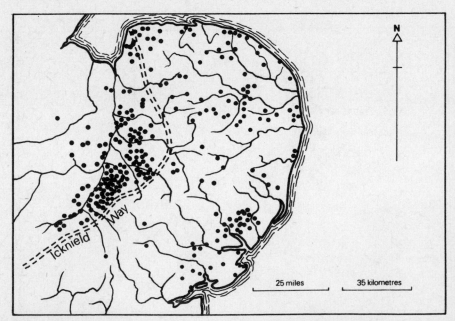

**Fig. 5 Distribution of Neolithic tools imported into East Anglia from other parts of Britain**

via Newmarket and Thetford. Beyond Thetford the Icknield Way swings northwards, but there is still no evidence of its prehistoric use, for here the delightful line of lanes, bridle paths and minor roads which runs almost straight as far as Wells-Next-The-Sea on the north Norfolk coast is in fact, at least in part, a Roman road.

If we look at other great routeways which, from the evidence of the stone axes, were certainly in use in Neolithic times, the situation is much the same. One is the so-called Pilgrims' Way of south-eastern England. Here again we can be sure that even in Neolithic times it was a major route from central Wessex into Kent. Yet today the section from Farnham to Guildford in Surrey is the main A31 road, a notoriously dangerous racetrack, while beyond Guildford, to the east, it becomes a wonderful succession of green lanes and by-roads. As we now see it, it is a mixture of medieval farm tracks and eighteenth-century and nineteenth-century access roads, so it is a good example of the basic rule concerning roads and tracks: that is, while keeping their general line they are continually altered over the centuries.

In recent years archaeologists have adapted the methods of looking

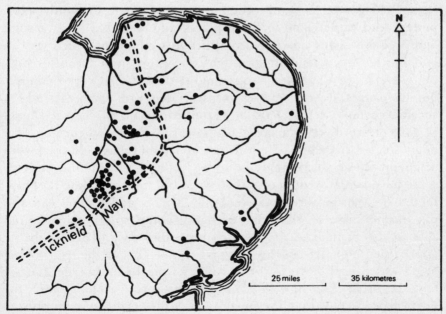

**Fig. 6 Distribution of Neolithic tools imported into East Anglia from Great Langdale in the lake District**

at stone axes and locating their origins and used them to examine the pottery of Neolithic people. This has had unexpected results. At a Neolithic site at Windmill Hill, near Avebury in Wiltshire, for example, though much of the pottery, as might have been expected, was made from locally obtainable clay, some was very different, for it contained minerals which only occur in Cornwall. As it is unlikely that Neolithic people carried around loads of clay, this must mean that the pots themselves had been made in the south-west peninsula and brought along trackways into Wiltshire.

The site of Windmill Hill itself is worth looking at in more detail for it also indicates another aspect of movement, and therefore the trackways, in this remote period. The site consists of a series of concentric rings of banks and ditches on a hill top, with gaps in the banks and causeways across the ditches. It is one of many such sites of the Neolithic period, usually called Causewayed Camps, which were clearly not defensive structures (because of the causeways) nor, as far as we can see, were they permanent settlements. Many of them are on hills, as at Windmill Hill; others, such as the one near Staines, Middlesex, lie on lowland. They appear to have been seasonal or annual meeting places, where farmers and traders met and exchanged goods, some of which came from afar. Certainly axes, pottery and cattle came to these places and were bartered or sold, and probably many other commodities as well, about which we can know little. Again, as with so much concerning these Neolithic people, we can see what was happening at these Causewayed Camps, but we cannot see the routeways associated with them. To take a specific example, let us look at Hambledon Hill in central Dorset (Fig. 7). Here there is a large Causewayed Camp on the top of a huge isolated chalk hill. The hillsides all round it have old trackways on them, but as always there is no way of dating them and, indeed, some have actually cut across the camp and must postdate it. Thus, though we can be sure that Neolithic farmers and traders came to this encampment regularly for perhaps centuries, at a date around 2800 BC, we cannot identify which path they took. They probably approached the hill from the east and climbed one of the two sloping spurs which lead down into the valley of the River Iwerne, but we have no proof. And how did the long-distance travellers reach the hill? Did they come from the south-west or the north along the crest of the great chalk escarpment? This is possible but unlikely, for the scarp face here is deeply eroded into coombes which would have

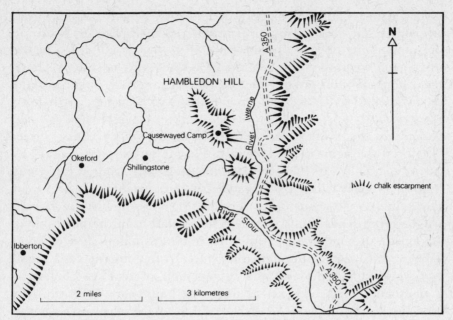

Fig. 7 Neolithic causewayed camp, Hambledon Hill, Dorset

made movement very difficult. Neolithic traders were much more likely to move along the foot of the escarpment where the gradients are much easier. Yet, if they did, then from the north they would have come along what is now the main A350 road from Blandford to Shaftesbury, while from the south-west they could only have traversed the line of present lanes which link the modern villages of Ibberton, Okeford and Shillingstone. Thus again we see both the impossibility of positively identifying the actual prehistoric trackways and the almost certain fact that we still use them today.

Finally in this examination of Neolithic trackways we must note the routes which led to the great 'temples' of this period. These huge constructions must have brought worshippers from near and far, but again their lines of approach are obscure. The greatest of these temples, Avebury in Wiltshire, illustrates this well. The enormous circular earthen bank and ditch with its inner array of stone circles was clearly the centre of a major religion (Fig. 8), yet where were the routeways that led to it? The allegedly prehistoric trackway called the The Ridgeway, which can be traced all the way from East Anglia as the Icknield Way and along the Berkshire Downs and the North Wiltshire Downs as The Ridgeway, approaches Avebury from the north but then completely ignores it and runs some two miles to the east on its way south. Though it may have been used by Neolithic worshippers, its present line does not show this at all well. On the other hand a number of other routeways actually meet at Avebury itself, none of which would be normally regarded as prehistoric at all. From the east is a rough cart track, which swings north from Marlborough, a few miles to the east, climbs over Fyfield Down, where lines of ruts are still visible, and runs into the Avebury Circle. Whatever its origins it was still in use in the seventeenth century as part of the main road between London and Bath, while the sections close to Avebury village itself are clearly recognizable as a field road of the eighteenth or nineteenth century. Even less prehistoric looking are the other roads into Avebury. One is that from the north along the upper Kennet valley, now the main Swindon-Devizes road (A361) which passes through the temple, while another is a small lane which runs south-east and becomes the present A4 London to Bath Road. These roads are as likely, perhaps more likely, to have been the Neolithic routes to Avebury than the mysterious ridgeway track which does not go there.

The story of man in Britain is marked around 3000 BC by new events. There may have been an influx of peoples, but there was certainly a technological revolution in that metal began to be used for tools. From then until the coming of the Roman armies in AD 43, many other developments can be seen in the archaeological record, and archaeologists have divided these centuries into various periods. The earliest is the Copper Age or Beaker Period from 3000 to perhaps 1800 BC, so called because of the use of copper tools and because the characteristic pottery made at this time consisted of highly decorated beaker-shaped vessels. This period was followed by the Bronze Age, the subdivisions of which need hardly concern us here, and was succeeded about 800 BC by what is known as the Iron Age, when this new metal started to replace bronze. From the point of view of the history of tracks all these complications are of little importance. What we have in general terms is a period of about 2000 years during which the population of Britain increased greatly and, as a result, the remaining forests were cleared and much of the country was settled, covered by villages and farms and cultivated for crops or grazed by cattle and sheep.

In the first few centuries after 2000 BC the population grew only slowly, but after about 1400 BC it began to rise rapidly so that, in the last two or three centuries before Roman times, the British Isles were in some respects over-populated. It is difficult for the non-archaeologist to realize this, for there is little in the present land-scape to suggest it; the gloomy picture of primitive painted men, eking a living on chalk or limestone hills, surrounded by impene-trable forests, lingers on from generation to generation of teachers and schoolchildren and thus into popular mythology. The reality was very different. In the area of north Bedfordshire and south North-amptonshire, where archaeological work has been very intensive, for example, we now know that around 200 BC there was an Iron Age farmstead, hamlet or village in every square mile of countryside. These were not on high, dry hills, or on level, well-drained gravel patches. They lay everywhere, in valleys, on hillsides, on clayland and on sandstone. The sites of numerous Iron Age farms have been discovered within the area of Salcey Forest, one of the great areas of woodland in southern Northamptonshire in the medieval period. These show clearly that in the late Iron Age this forest did not exist, or at least not in its medieval form. Such later prehistoric settlements which are now being discovered in every part of Britain were

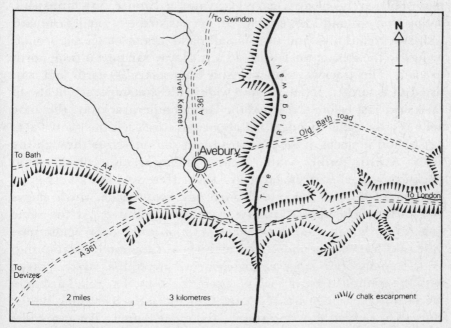

Fig. 8 Neolithic 'temple', Avebury, Wiltshire

surrounded by fields of various types. Those used mainly for arable purposes were small rectangular paddocks, bounded by low banks, ditches, walls or hedges. In addition larger areas, delimited by banks and ditches, were used for grazing animals while in certain areas, notably in parts of Wessex, huge tracts of countryside, up for four miles across and also bounded by large banks and ditches, were used as 'ranches'.

Through these fields, leading from village to farmstead and from farmstead to the pastures, were trackways. Few of them remain on the ground today, for later activity has removed all trace, but on certain soils and in suitable conditions, some of them, together with their associated fields, farmsteads, hamlets and villages, are visible from the air (Plate I). As a result of intensive survey all over Britain, many hundreds of miles of these trackways are now known. It is not often that any one track can be traced over very long distances, because of the later activities and limitations caused by soils and crop conditions, but what has been found indicates that over large parts of Britain there was, certainly by about 500 BC, a very complex pattern of trackways. Let us now look at some of these.

High on the chalk downlands of Dorset, at a place called Shearplace Hill, archaeologists have excavated a Bronze Age farmstead, dating from around 1300 BC (Fig. 9). It consisted of a small farmyard with two round huts and some small paddocks or closes set around it. Just to the west of the farmstead a trackway ran past it from north to south. This trackway was traceable from some 700 yards and consisted of a terrace about six feet wide with contemporary fields on each side; just before it reached the farm another trackway, this time hollowed by traffic to a depth of about three feet, left the main track, passed to the north of the farmstead and ran on across through the fields. A little further south, another holloway also left the main trackway and entered the farmyard itself. Here we have a very good example of a small piece of Bronze Age countryside which shows how farms, fields and trackways were all integrated. At the same time, even though there is evidence here for a trackway whose purpose is at least partly understood and whose situation in relationship to its contemporary landscape is clear, we are still, as always, faced with the continued use of such a system of tracks. The relationship of the farm to the main track is such that the track itself may be the older. The farmstead was certainly abandoned after a few years, the fields may have been too, but the tracks probably went on being used for centuries. Indeed the excavation revealed evidence that Romano-British people, probably shepherds, stayed for a short time on the site, and they at least must have used the trackway. Certainly later people also used these same tracks, including farmers in this century. So, once again, we must ask ourselves what is the real date of such a trackway?

This same problem recurs every time we look at these late prehistoric trackways. In a very different part of the country, At Achurch, near Oundle, in Northamptonshire, aerial photography has revealed

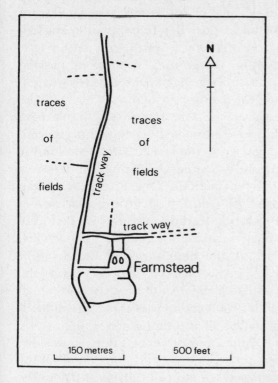

traces

of

fields

traces

of

fields

track way

track way

Farmstead

150 metres    500 feet

Fig. 9 Bronze Age farmstead, trackways and fields, Shearplace Hill, Dorset

a remarkable series of early occupation sites, visible from the air as a result of changes in the crop colour (Fig. 10). The main part of the site, the generally rectangular arrangement of paddocks, is an Iron Age village dating from around 300 BC. The circular marks are the positions of small round huts. A trackway, shown as two parallel lines, in fact marking the deliberately dug side ditches, can be seen approaching the village from the north, passing through it and then running on across the fields to the south. Here again we have an integrated system of tracks, this time of the Iron Age. However, further south the trackway passes a group of enclosures attached to its west side. This is another settlement, probably a farmstead, but of the Roman period rather than the Iron Age, probably dating from between AD 200 and 300. As both Iron Age village and Roman farm are attached to the main track, presumably the inhabitants of both used it, so it is not just a prehistoric track but a Roman road as well.

Back in southern England, extensive excavations have been carried out on a site at Owselbury near Winchester, in Hampshire, which have shown how even highly skilled archaeologists find it difficult to explain the complex history of trackways associated with prehistoric and Roman farms and fields. Before excavation started, crop marks of ditched tracks, visible only from the air, and deeply cut holloways, which still exist on the ground, seem to be passing through contemporary fields into an Iron Age farmstead. However, a more complex picture was revealed after excavation which, in the end, was not really understood at all. The apparently simple Iron Age farmstead turned out to be a continuously occupied place from early Iron Age times, around 500 BC, to the late Roman period in the fourth century AD. Further, the seemingly clear-cut patterns of trackways belong to many different periods. One Roman track ran over the filled-in ditch of part of the Iron Age farmyard. A section of another ditched trackway, apparently leading into the late Iron Age farmyard and traceable through contemporary fields for over 250 yards, was quarried away early in the Roman period and thus put out of use. An additional discovery was at least one other trackway, which continued in use up until the nineteenth century and which ran across the whole area. With problems such as these, the difficulties of establishing the exact details of the thousands of prehistoric trackways become immense. And because excavation is a slow, expensive and time-consuming process only a tiny fraction of all the known tracks will ever be examined scientifically. In most places the archaeologists can only guess the date and period of use of the trackways they discover.

Some of the best apparently prehistoric trackways associated with farms and hamlets lie in the north of England on the high moorlands and fellsides. At Crosby Garret near Appleby, in Cumbria, for example, is a beautifully preserved prehistoric village with stone wall yards, house foundations and small paddocks, surrounded by rectangular fields (Fig. 11). Two parallel walled tracks enter the village from the west, while a broad droveway runs east down the

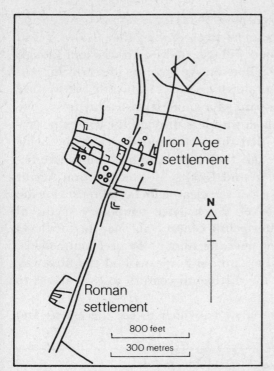

Fig. 10 Iron Age and
Roman settlement and
track, Thorpe Achurch,
Northamptonshire

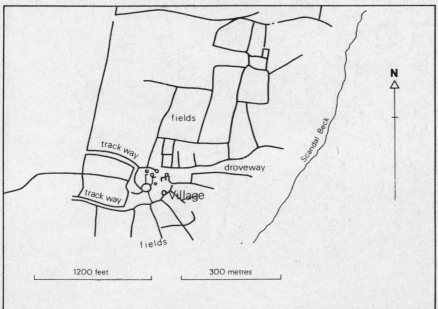

Fig. 11 Prehistoric village, trackways and fields, Crosby Garret, Cumbria

hillside, presumably for the purpose of taking animals between the adjacent fields down to the Scandal Beck in the valley below. Yet in fact we do not know the date of village, fields or tracks and though they are certainly Iron Age or Roman, we have no idea which.

Back in Dorset, on the high downland at Turnworth, we can see clearly the circular enclosure bank of a small farmstead lying on one side of a ditched trackway which wanders through the contemporary fields. Here we can be sure that the farm, and therefore the fields and track, are all prehistoric but they may date from anywhere between the early Bronze Age, around 1800 BC, to the late Iron Age at around 100 BC. Here again we can see clear evidence of reuse, for the prehistoric fields bear traces of much later temporary medieval ploughing, probably of the thirteenth century AD. Yet the medieval plough marks, though running over the sides of the prehistoric fields, stop short of the trackway. This probably means that the trackway itself was still being used in the thirteenth century to gain access to the arable land of that date.

Dorset is an especially fine area in which to see the extent and

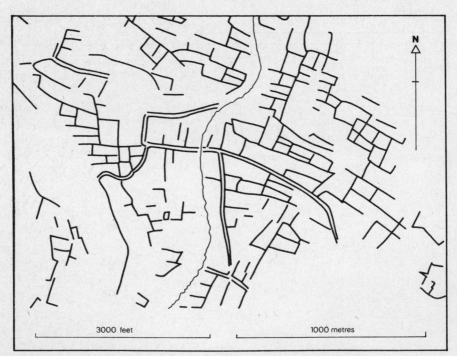

Fig. 12 Prehistoric trackways and fields, Dole's Hill, Dorset

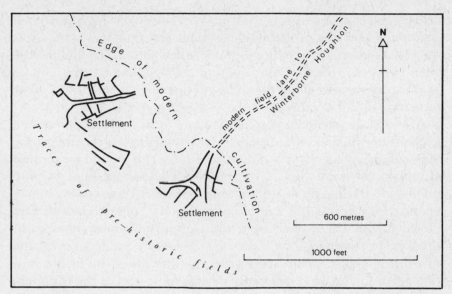

Fig. 13 Prehistoric settlements, fields and trackways, Winterbourne Houghton, Dorset

complexity of prehistoric trackways because archaeologists have
examined them more carefully than in other places. We can therefore
accept that what has been revealed in Dorset also existed over much of
Britain at that time. Some of the trackways which have come to light
are truly remarkable, such as those on Dole's Hill, near Puddle-
town. There, lying across a narrow chalk valley, is a complicated
arrangement of routes, sometimes wandering through the prehistoric
fields, but in other places changing direction sharply at field corners.
(Fig. 12). Not far away, at Winterbourne Houghton, parts of two
systems still exist. One (Fig. 13) has a prehistoric farmstead from
which a narrow embanked holloway runs east through the small
fields of the farm. On the next hillside is a larger settlement,
probably a village, set around a triangular 'green', and from each
corner of the green trackways run out into the fields. This example
is of particular interest in that the north-eastern trackway ends
at a modern hedge, beyond which medieval and modern cultivation have removed all trace. However, the line of the trackway itself
is continued down the hill into the village of Winterbourne Houghton by a modern field lane. This lane is ostensibly of early
nineteenth-century date and was made in 1805 when the existing

fields were laid out in order to give access to the high downland pasture; in fact it is probably much older and thus may actually be the prehistoric track, running into the valley bottom. In this case the main street of Winterbourne Houghton village, and its continuation as the modern road along the valley to the next village, is also likely to be prehistoric in origin.

At this stage one must exercise caution, for it is easy to go on and explain the whole modern road system as being largely prehistoric. While this may be so, we cannot prove it – yet it should be continually borne in mind that it is possible. The picture of these later prehistoric trackways, as we are able to recover them today, is staggering. It is clear that by the end of prehistoric times almost all parts of the British Isles, apart from the highest and most inhospitable hills, were criss-crossed by trackways. Therefore we may accept that many, if not most, of the main roads, country lanes and bridle paths that we use today were originally developed as part of the communication system of an intensively settled and farmed later prehistoric landscape.

Another localized group of trackways, which is known to have existed in the Bronze and Iron Ages, is situated in the Somerset Levels. Tracks, almost identical to the heavy Neolithic trackways described earlier, have been discovered there running across the marshland linking the islands to the uplands. They show the continuing ability of these prehistoric people to create sophisticated methods of road construction if the need arose.

So far we have looked at these later prehistoric tracks in a local context, that is, we have assumed that their development and use was a result of local agricultural and social needs. Yet, just as in the Neolithic period, when there was extensive long-distance trade in stone axes, pottery and in unknown goods, the Bronze Age and Iron Age people continued to demand commodities which had to be transported over long distances. Indeed the variety of materials moved around the country increased markedly towards the end of prehistoric times. Once again it is impossible to identify much of what was undoubtedly traded but objects made of durable materials have survived and give us some idea of what was happening. The most important of the commodities that were traded all over Britain in both the Bronze Age and the Iron Age were the very materials that gave these periods their names. The advantages that bronze tools had over the earlier stone ones, and then the superiority of iron tools over bronze, meant that as soon as a knowledge of these metals was acquired they were in great demand. However the sources of tin and copper that went to make bronze were few and located in specific areas. Likewise, though the ores needed to produce iron are much more widespread, they still had a restricted distribution and thus the demand for iron created trade from these areas to customers. The development of the bronze industry in prehistoric times is as yet not clearly understood. Certainly the actual sources of the tin and copper have not been accurately located, yet it is certain that the ores occur in only a few places and even if all these were exploited in prehistoric times the refined ores, or the finished tools, then had to be transported long distances. It is very difficult to locate the actual mines; the veins worked must have been shallow and inevitably these are the ones that later peoples also worked.

The major source of copper, not only for the British Isles but for large parts of western Europe, seems to have been southern Ireland, where there are easily accessible deposits. Other probable places are in Argyll in Scotland, perhaps in Cheshire, on the Lizard Peninsula in Cornwall and in north Wales close to Llandudno. Tin, the other metal needed for bronze, is more rare. Perhaps the major source of tin for most of Europe and beyond in prehistoric times was Cornwall, though southern Ireland again is another possible area. Here at once we see a basic need for trade, for having abstracted the ores and refined them, the copper and tin had to be brought together to make bronze tools before the tools themselves could be traded.

Bronze tools, produced from these various sources of ores, are of course known from every corner of Britain: the total number runs into many thousands and all imply movement of either traders or smiths along tracks. We do know something of the organization of this trade and industry from careful examination of the many finds. The production of a number of bronze tools is a fairly sophisticated craft, so it seems that the task was, in the main, left to itinerant metal workers who travelled all over the country, carrying a few ingots of bronze, a quantity of broken or discarded tools, moulds and their own tools for cutting, trimming and finishing. As they moved from farm to village to hamlet, the occupants would order what they required and the smith would build a small furnace and produce the tools on the spot. In return, as part payment, old implements would be handed over to be melted down and recast for the customers in the next village.

The introduction of iron working into Britain, perhaps in the sixth century BC, led to the rapid use of iron on a large scale and thus to increasing trade in metal. However, iron ore in Britain is not only widespread, but relatively easy to obtain. In the Forest of Dean, for example, the ores could actually be picked up on the surface of the ground or, at the most, gained from shallow surface diggings; the same applies to the extensive iron ore deposits in the Weald of south-east England. Other places where iron was obtainable without difficulty were in Northamptonshire, Lincolnshire and North Yorkshire, but there were also many other small local sources that could be and probably were exploited. At the Iron Age village found at All Cannings Cross in the Vale of Pewsey, in Wiltshire, for instance, the inhabitants who made iron tools in front of their houses, to judge from the slag and iron ore discovered there, probably obtained the material from the Lower Greensand deposits less than ten miles away. Thus the movement of iron ores and iron tools was probably carried out over much shorter distances than the earlier bronze trade. On the other hand it was certainly much more intensive.

Another metal, also used and certainly much prized by prehistoric people as by all men, was gold. Again the sources of gold are very limited. In prehistoric times Ireland as well as Wales provided the main supplies, and gold was traded widely all over the country. Indeed, in the early Bronze Age, trade in gold is often said to have been the basis of an incredible rich and sophisticated society that emerged in southern Britain with its centre in Wessex. There, in Wiltshire and Dorset, but with outliers as far away as Cornwall, Sussex, Northamptonshire and East Anglia, the archaeologists have discovered the immensely rich burials of a people who used gold on a considerable scale. It was fashioned into buckles and brooches, decorated dagger handles and even gold cups. Some archaeologists have suggested that these people controlled the movement of gold and bronze from Ireland and Wales to the continent, and that certain objects buried with their dead show that they were not only in close contact with people in other parts of Britain but also those in France, central Europe and even Scandinavia.

Trans-continental trade of this kind was not confined to the early Bronze Age alone, though it was perhaps at its most spectacular then. It occurred all through prehistoric times. Even in the Neolithic period the stone axes produced in Britain were sent across the Channel and other axes, made in France, found their way into this country. And all through the Bronze and Iron Ages goods came into and went from Britain to western Europe. In the latter part of the Iron Age, in the century before the Roman conquest, the trade with Europe was of a kind which has given archaeologists an insight into the nature of Iron Age society. In East Anglia, Mediterranean wine jars have been found in the burials of people who were presumably rich chieftains and they show just how complex and sophisticated late prehistoric trade could be. Obviously these jars were imported into Britain containing wine and presumably they arrived by ship but they must have reached their final destination, at places such as Thaxted in Essex, Welwyn in Hertfordshire, Snailswell in Cambridgeshire and Cambridge itself, overland and in some considerable quantity. While packhorse transport is the most likely way of moving this kind of commodity, we must remember that by this time, wheeled carts existed. Certainly war chariots were used in battle, but from our point of view some of the carts such as those found in Iron Age burials in Yorkshire are of more consequence in that they show that heavy wheeled transport was in use at this time. This of course implies the presence of well-made tracks to go with them.

Our final piece of evidence for late Iron Age long-distance trade is a written source for, at this time, as the wine jars show, Britain was in contact with the expanding Roman Empire. The classical author Strabo listed the exports of Britain immediately prior to the Roman Conquest; they included corn, cattle, gold, hides and hunting dogs as well as slaves. All these, except perhaps the last two, would need clearly defined roads, and in the case of corn and perhaps hides wheeled transport to move them to the coasts.

So again we return, inevitably, to the identification of the long-distance roads along which the gold, iron, corn, hides and cattle were moved in the latter part of the prehistoric period. And again our eyes settle on the traditional prehistoric trackways of Britain. These figure so largely in our maps, in most of the literature on tracks and in popular history that whatever the problems they pose we cannot ignore them. Let us look at these once more. The basic problem is to see why we think of them as prehistoric. The view that the great ridgeways were prehistoric trackways grew up in the early years of archaeological studies when certain features became apparently obvious, the main one being that most of the visible remains of prehistoric occupation were on the higher open areas of Britain. The vast majority of Bronze Age burial mounds, Iron Age farms and forts as well as prehistoric field systems could be actually seen on the downlands of Wessex, on the moorlands of south-west England, on the Pennine edges, or over the chalk wolds of east Yorkshire. It was therefore assumed that throughout prehistoric times most people lived in these areas. This idea was given initial support by the fact that little, apart from odd finds of stone axes and bronze tools, was found in the lower areas of the country where the soils were on heavy clay, or where great rivers wound their ways through deep valleys to the sea. The picture was interpreted as meaning that most of this lowland area was covered with dense forest and extensive marshes where primitive upland people rarely penetrated – and from this it followed that when these people wanted to move from one dry upland area to another they would obviously tend to follow the natural ridgeways which led through the ubiquitous forests. Thus the chalk ridgeways radiating outwards from Wessex seemed to be the only logical ways these people could have moved. When the ridge-ways were studied it became even clearer that these routes were of prehistoric date, for all along them was visible evidence for prehis-toric activity, such as burial mounds and forts. As a result early archaeologists had no doubt that the chalk ridgeways and escarp-ments of southern England were the major routes of prehistoric times. Once the concept was established, it was then easy for other trackways to be discovered, and the literature of roads is full of them. One example of these, important because it was recognized by some of the foremost archaeologists of our time in 1940, is the Jurassic Way.

The identification of this route across England from the Humber to the Bristol Channel was based partly on geological considerations, as it follows the main outcrop of Jurassic limestone, and partly on the known distribution of objects and sites largely dated to the later prehistoric period. It was thus seen as a prehistoric trackway mainly used in the Iron Age. With hindsight we can now see that the evidence for a real trackway was very slight, and that of Iron Age date slighter still. Nevertheless, at the time, and with the information at the disposal of the archaeologists, it seemed a fine example of an early trackway. To illustrate how the Jurassic Way was identified, let us examine in more detail the part of it which crosses Northamp-tonshire from Banbury to Stamford (Figs. 14 and 15).

Between these two places is an area of Jurassic rocks, much of it forming high, dry land. The track was said to run from Banbury via two alternative routes. The southern one is marked by a wandering second-class road which passes along the watershed between the River Tove and its tributaries on the east and the Cherwell and its tributaries to the west, crosses the Watling Street (A5) south of Weedon and runs into Northampton. From there the Way ran north on one or both sides of a small south-flowing stream, largely on dry Northampton Sandstone hills as far as the small market town of Desborough. The alternative route from Banbury lay further north-west and ran across the headwaters of the Cherwell as far as Daventry. It then crossed the line of the Watling Street at Watford and climbed onto the hills again to reach Desborough. From there the Way ran on north-east along the crest of the limestone escarpment above the River Welland, finally crossing the latter at Stamford. Worked out on a small-scale map, sitting in a comfortable room, this may seem an excellent line for a prehistoric routeway. But actually followed on the ground, even today, it becomes far less attractive. For the first ten miles or so from Banbury on the main route it is reasonable, but thereafter, as far as Northampton, it traverses no less than eight broad, wet, clay-lined valleys of south-east flowing streams before the difficult task of crossing the wide valley of the River Nene at Northampton. Beyond, though the hills to the north seem to be dry and sandy, the route has to cross a number of deep valleys before reaching the high land south of Desborough. The alternative route via Daventry is much worse for there the whole country is broken up into deep valleys and high, steep-sided hills until well to the north-east of Watford. Beyond Desborough the route along the top of the limestone escarpment is much more feasible, though it is of some interest that there is no continuous modern road at all in this area. The existing main road, the Oxford-Northampton-Stamford trunk road (A43) lies well to the south-east, while the nearest continuous road lies at the base of the scarp face in the Welland valley. On the assumption that in prehistoric times the lower parts of this Northamptonshire landscape were thickly wooded and largely impassable, then the alleged Jurassic Way was in itself a difficult and dangerous route to follow.

The archaeological evidence for the use of the Jurassic Way in later prehistoric times was little enough in this part of Northamptonshire in 1940. Between Banbury and Northampton a single Bronze Age burial mound was known, on the line of the Way itself, though five miles to the north-west of it at one point an Iron Age hill fort,

Arbury Camp, and six miles to the south at another point a further
fort, Rainsborough, were also well known. At Northampton itself
was yet another fort, Hunsbury. This latter fort enhanced the idea of
a Jurassic Way, for the pottery found there is identical to pottery
discovered in south Gloucestershire and Somerset and thus it seemed
likely it had come to Hunsbury via the Jurassic Way. North of
Northampton, an alleged Neolithic long barrow lay on the line of the
Way at Pitsford, while eight miles further on the discovery, during
the building of an airfield in 1940, of an Iron Age farmstead at
Draughton, almost on the line of the Way, seemed to confirm the
existence of the route here. At Desborough one of the most famous of
all Iron Age finds in Britain, a remarkable highly decorated bronze
mirror, was additional proof. Along the alternative line of the
Jurassic Way, via Daventry, there seemed to be two Iron Age forts,
one at Arbury Hill, south of Daventry, and Borough Hill, one of the
largest hill forts in Britain to the east. Beyond Desborough nothing
of prehistoric date was known until the Jurassic Way passed far
beyond the Northamptonshire boundary (Fig. 14). Put in the
perhaps crude terms employed here, the archaeological evidence was

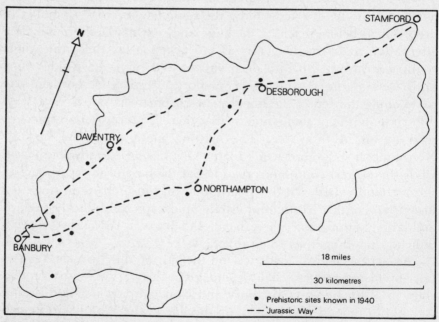

Fig. 14 The Jurassic Way in Northamptonshire: 1940

weak. But it is made weaker by recent research. It is now known
that Arbury Hill, south of Daventry, is not a hill fort at all, while the
Neolithic long barrow at Pitsford is probably a Saxon burial place.

Thus the real evidence for a prehistoric track along the Jurassic
Way, at least in Northamptonshire even in 1940, seems difficult to
find. It is made largely worthless by the additional evidence of prehistoric settlement which has been found in the area over the last few
years. Numerous new settlement sites of the later prehistoric period
have come to light as a result of aerial photography and detailed
ground examination all over Northamptonshire, not only on the dry
hills, but in the clay valleys as well. Some are close to the alleged Way
but most are quite unrelated to it. Some of those visible on air
photographs show clearly that they had their own ditched trackways
associated with them (Fig. 10) and their siting, origins and continued
existence had nothing to do with the Jurassic Way, whether it ever
existed or not. These settlements were part of the intensive occupation which covered almost the entire county in later prehistoric
times.

This detailed examination of the Jurassic Way and its relegation

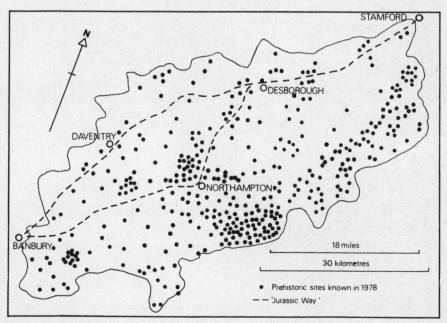

Fig. 15 The Jurassic Way in Northamptonshire: 1978

to a position of possible non-existence will not, of course, alter the view of the confirmed 'prehistoric trackway' supporters. They will no doubt say, and with some justification, that such a way is a poor example to choose and that the chalk ridgeways of southern England are much better in that they show clearly that the density of pre-historic occupation along them is of a far higher level than that of the hill forts every ten or fifteen miles along the Jurassic Way. And indeed this is so, but it does not prove anything. If we look at a 'real' prehistoric trackway we can see this well. No one would doubt that the so-called Icknield Way in south-east Cambridgeshire is a superb example of a prehistoric track: it crosses the county from Newmarket to Royston and is on an almost continuous line of dry chalkland between the fens to the north and the heavy clays to the south. Here there are no steep hills, clay valleys or other obstacles to block the way. The only major features which interrupt its line are the two branches of the River Cam which cross it at right angles south of Cambridge, but these small streams in wide, easily crossed valleys, could never have provided problems for the long-distance traveller. And there is plenty of evidence for prehistoric activity along its line

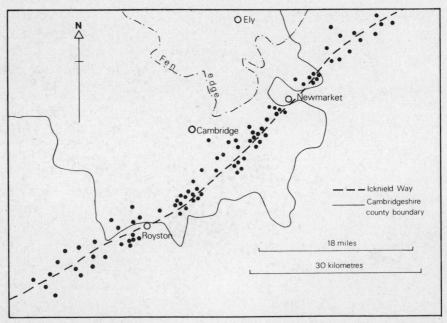

Fig. 16 The Icknield Way, Cambridgeshire: prehistoric sites along the Way

here for the prehistoric trackway devotees. The modern 1:25,000 os map marks one hill fort and seventeen prehistoric burial mounds on or very close to the Icknield Way. If we go to the standard work on Cambridgeshire archaeology (C. Fox, *Archaeology of the Cambridge Region*, 1923), we find that there are many more sites known along the Way, amounting to fifty-six prehistoric burials, the hill fort and an Iron Age farm. These, when plotted on a map of the Icknield Way, look impressive (Fig. 16). However it is not as easy as this. We have to look at all the archaeological sites in the surrounding area, discovered over recent years by detailed field examination, air photography and excavation. This is difficult, for much of the information is buried in archives and is not readily understood. Yet this evidence must be used if the real importance of the Icknield Way is to be assessed.

When all this new information is plotted on the same map (Fig. 17), a very different impression emerges which indicates that there were other factors controlling the location of prehistoric occupation besides the Icknield Way. It appears that the fen edges and the river valleys were far more suitable for settlement than the high

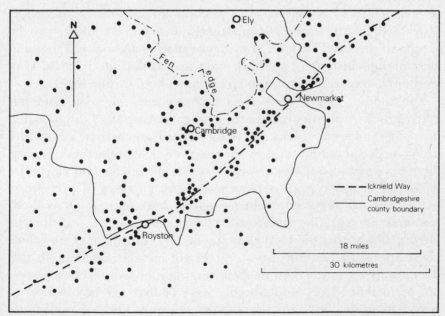

Fig. 17 The Icknield Way, Cambridgeshire: all known prehistoric sites

chalk downland and that there must have been routes along the edges of the fen and down the valleys linking these prehistoric sites. We probably still use these roads today.

However the situation is even more complicated than this. Our knowledge of the burial mounds along the Way is directly related to the land use of the area, not in prehistoric times but in the historic period. For from early medieval times, and perhaps long before, right up to the nineteenth century this dry chalk downland was permanent grassland grazed by sheep. The lower land along the fen edge and in the river valleys was permanent arable land, in which the yearly turning of the plough inevitably destroyed or flattened all traces of ancient occupation. Thus the fifty-six burial mounds along the line of the Icknield Way give a distorted impression of prehistoric occupation, for they are only the survivals of the past, not the total picture. And indeed modern techniques have shown this. Air photographs taken of the land along the fen edges and in the river valleys have revealed many new prehistoric occupation sites which were quite invisible on the ground. In one of the fen-edge villages, for example, an air photograph shows the dark ring of the ditch of a Bronze Age burial mound in the back garden of a house, while in a single large field on the edge of the River Cam, well to the north of the Icknield Way, a vast array of ditches, and enclosures, as well as at least two farmsteads, all apparently of prehistoric date, can be seen from the air. This kind of evidence shows only too well the total amount of prehistoric occupation and suggests that the Icknield Way was not as important as it appears to have been at first sight.

The concept of the survival of archaeological sites on land not utilized by later peoples is important when looking at all the so-called prehistoric ridgeway tracks. All of them were largely used for pasture in the medieval period, and so the relatively few prehistoric remains there have survived to the present day. In the valleys and clay vales below the ridgeways, as well as elsewhere, all trace of prehistoric occupation was removed centuries ago by later farmers. Now modern aerial photography and detailed field examination reveal the true picture, illustrating the total exploitation and settlement of the whole landscape in prehistoric times. Again we must stress that all this does not mean, in the final analysis, that our ancient trackways were not prehistoric. They undoubtedly were of that age but instead of seeing them as the main or perhaps the only lines of prehistoric communication, we should look at them as being only one part of a highly complicated pattern of routes which stretched into every corner of Britain in the centuries before the Roman conquest. If this is so, we see our prehistoric ancestors in a more kindly light as a sophisticated people, more involved in the day-to-day practicalities of farming and trading than in the laying out of mysterious lines of communication across the dark country.

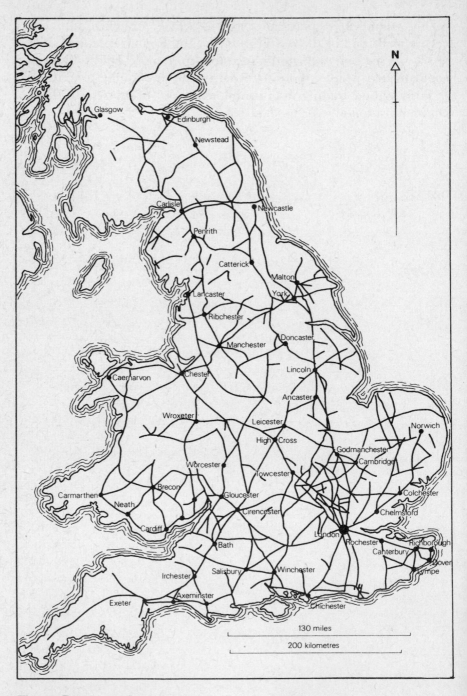

Fig. 18 Roman roads in Britain

# 2 Roman Roads and Trackways

In AD 43, the Roman armies landed in south-east England and, moving north and west, rapidly conquered the south-eastern part of the British Isles. Then after a short halt they moved on so that by AD 83 all Wales, northern England and the lowlands of Scotland were in Roman hands. The final military frontier, Hadrian's Wall, was constructed and completed about AD 130 and soon after the Antonine Wall, between the Clyde and the Forth, was completed. At this point the Romans seemed to have overreached themselves and, as a result of disturbances and attacks on their troops both behind and outside the walls, were forced to withdraw from Scotland and establish the final northern frontier along Hadrian's Wall. Thus most of Britain lay within the bounds of the Roman Empire and was given the trappings of the civilized world. Among the most impressive of these were the great roads which are still so much a feature of the landscape.

However we must remind ourselves of the nature of the country that was taken into the empire. As we saw in the last chapter, by the time the Roman invasions took place the landscape was tamed, cultivated and grazed, criss-crossed by thousands of miles of lanes and tracks and travelled by a sophisticated people who had learned to control their environment to a large extent. This was the land and the people that now came under Roman domination.

The aim of the Romans in taking over this country was threefold. Firstly, there was the pursuit of political aggrandizement, and secondly the desire for new land to tax and exploit to increase the wealth of Rome. But there was also an ideological basis, not to be ignored or hidden by the more obvious political and economic aims. The Romans genuinely believed that by bringing Roman civilization to the benighted people on the edges of the known world they were achieving their destiny. These three aims, when combined with an

41

almost unstoppable military machine, a highly developed bureau-
cracy, a keen sense for economic exploitation and the, by prehistoric
standards, extremely high level of technology, architecture, agriculture and obvious material comforts, changed the attitudes and way
of life of the British people they conquered almost overnight. Towns
were planned and populated, local and national government was set
up, exports flourished, agriculture was improved, industry was
developed or encouraged, living standards rose and permanent peace
was established. Most important of all, a new communications
system to link the towns, speed military traffic, move exports, send
messages and transport new industrial products was laid out across the
newly conquered land (Fig. 18).

Much of this new road system which, once established, lasted for
three to four hundred years, and indeed is still partly in use today,
was created for purely military purposes connected with the initial
invasion and the subsequent conquest. In addition a series of later
roads was constructed for what one may call general economic
reasons associated with the post-conquest exploitation and civilization of Britain, as well as hundreds of miles of purely local roads.
The military roads were of course not only the earliest, but in many
respects the most important. It is at these we must first look.

During the initial conquest of south-east Britain in AD 43, the
Roman army probably moved along existing Iron Age trackways as
it advanced across the countryside. But it was a large army, consisting of four legions as well as substantial groups of auxiliary troops –
at least 40,000 men and probably considerably more – who had to
be supplied with food, equipment and reinforcements as well as supported by a well-integrated communications system. As the army
moved, therefore, it had to be followed closely by road builders and,
in addition, roads were constructed by the army as part of both the
tactical and strategic plans developed for controlling and defending
blocks of conquered territory. Thus the military roads of Roman Britain are of two kinds, those for communication and supply and those
for the control of conquered areas. Of course many roads performed
both functions, but it is important to see how the two kinds were
developed and used.

The original invasion force landed on the east Kent coast, with
Richborough as its base. The initial landing was followed by an
advance to the London area, making the Roman road from Richborough via Canterbury and Rochester to London perhaps the

earliest of all our Roman roads. Additional roads in east Kent from Dover and Lympne to Canterbury may also be early ones linking other supply ports with the main route to London. From London the army moved north-east to Colchester, then the main Iron Age capital in south-east England, which was soon captured. Again the main London-Chelmsford-Colchester Roman road, which must have followed this advance, is probably an early one. At Colchester the army appears to have been divided into its legionary components. One legion, the Twentieth, remained at Colchester, probably for political reasons, and perhaps part of this legion was dispatched north to subdue the rest of East Anglia. The story is not clear, but if this indeed happened then it is possible that the two main roads of the area, the one from Colchester to Norwich and the other north across Suffolk and west Norfolk to the shores of the Wash, may represent this advance. The Ninth Legion moved north-west along the south side of the fens and marched north to Lincoln, where a major permanent fortress was established. The line of this movement is not only marked by forts at Cambridge, Godmanchester, near Peterborough and at Ancaster, but by the Roman road from Colchester via Cambridge to Godmanchester and then north along what is known as the Ermine Street to Lincoln. The third of the four legions, the Fourteenth, was given the task of subduing the south-east Midlands and therefore advanced north-west from London and Godmanchester. Behind them the road engineers laid out Watling Street, probably as far as High Cross in Leicestershire, and what we now call the Gartree Road from Godmanchester to Leicester. The last of the legions, the Second, was sent south-west from London. Here the closeness of the south coast meant that ships could well help with supplies. In addition, as the Iron Age tribe occupying Sussex gave in to the Romans without a fight, no coast road seems to have been needed for some way. As a result the main road which followed the Second Legion was probably the London-Reading-Salisbury road which was then extended to Dorchester. From there it was pushed west into Devon to reach the final army post at that time, Exeter. Then the Second Legion turned back and moved north-east to Gloucester where it linked up with the Fourteenth Legion moving south-west from Leicester.

All this was achieved by AD 47 and at that stage a frontier was established between the newly conquered land of south-east England and the defiant Iron Age peoples of the north-west, running from

Exeter to Lincoln via Axminster, Cirencester and Gloucester. Along this line a frontier road, the Foss Way, was constructed both for use by military patrols and for communications with numerous forts. However, the new frontier was not a stable one and though it was apparently hoped to be a permanent line, very soon the armies had to advance beyond it. The Fourteenth Legion was sent forward across the west Midlands to Wroxeter near Shrewsbury and the Watling Street followed it. The Twentieth Legion was brought from Colchester to Gloucester and from there moved on into the Welsh Marches. Soon afterwards a series of roads linking the northern and southern flanks of this advance appeared through Hereford and Worcester as well as elsewhere. At the same time the Second Legion was probably pushing on across Devon and Cornwall where a major road perhaps marks the line of its advance.

The intricate pattern of roads, particularly in the south-east corner of Wales, around Monmouth, Abergavenny and Usk, probably reflects the long drawn-out struggle of the Roman armies along the Welsh borders at this time, for the final submission of the area was not achieved until AD 60. It is probable that the land had to be conquered and then divided into blocks bounded by roads along the valleys or the ridge tops, in order to check the subsequent guerilla warfare which developed. Nevertheless it was finally achieved and plans for a further advance into north Wales put into operation. But the Boudiccan rebellion in East Anglia at this time had to be put down and this, and other outside political events in Rome itself, held up the conquest of the rest of Britain for nearly ten years.

In AD 70 a new campaign opened. The Ninth Legion advanced from Lincoln to York where a new fortress was established and parts of east Yorkshire were conquered. As a result the Ermine Street was extended north from Lincoln, across the Humber and on to York. In addition, it is probable that the intensive pattern of roads, radiating from the fortress built at this time at Malton, north-east of York, at least in part reflects the same military strategy of control in newly conquered land that we saw in south-east Wales.

With York and east Yorkshire held, the Romans turned to Wales and between AD 70 and 79 most of that country passed under Roman rule. Probably aided by coastal landings, troops marched through the whole of Wales and, in addition to constructing at least twenty forts, they quickly covered the country with a network of roads. Though many of these are probably still undiscovered, the picture as we have it in south Wales, for example, is probably typical. There was a coast road from the new legionary fortress at Caerleon, via Cardiff and Neath to Carmarthen, while other roads were driven into the uplands along the valleys or over the ridges between them from the forts on the coast to the forts at Brecon, Llandovery, Llanio, Clyro, Abergavenny, Y Gaer, Usk and Gelligaer (Fig. 19). Yet again we see the basic military purpose of these roads, to gain and keep control of the newly conquered area by providing good communications for constant patrolling by army units based on regularly spaced forts.

In AD 77, with Wales still not quite conquered, Agricola became governor of Britain. He completed the subjection of Wales with a campaign along the coast to Anglesey, based on a new fortress at Chester. This led to the construction both of the coastal road from the latter place and of others through the deep valleys of Snowdonia, again accompanied by forts. Then in AD 79 Agricola started the final attack on the north of Britain which was carried out with remarkable speed within two years. Though the details are not known with certainty, the excavation of the numerous forts associated with this

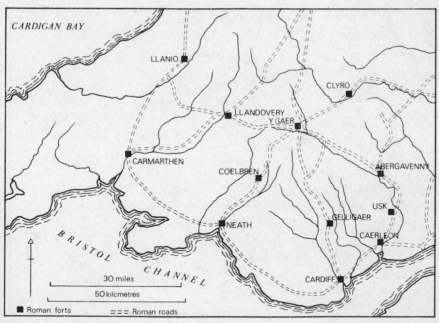

Fig. 19 Roman forts and roads in south Wales

campaign, together with the knowledge of the contemporary roads, indicate how the military situation developed and show the importance of the road system in its success.

The army seems to have driven north in two columns, one along the western side of the Pennines from Chester and the other on the east from York. Each advance is marked by main roads, from Chester via Manchester, Ribchester, Penrith and Carlisle, and from York via Catterick to Corbridge on the Tyne. At the same time link roads were cut across the Pennines to join the two advances, so breaking up the mountains into controllable blocks. These link roads include that from Manchester to Doncaster, Ribchester to York and Penrith to Catterick (Fig. 20). The Lake District perhaps suffered the same fate at this time with at least two roads being cut right across it.

In the following years AD 81–2, the armies continued north into southern Scotland, still on two fronts until the Clyde-Forth isthmus was reached. The western road ran north from Carlisle as far as Glasgow, while the eastern one was extended to the area of Edinburgh. Again link roads were cut across the Southern Uplands. The year after the army moved north again, though now the geography

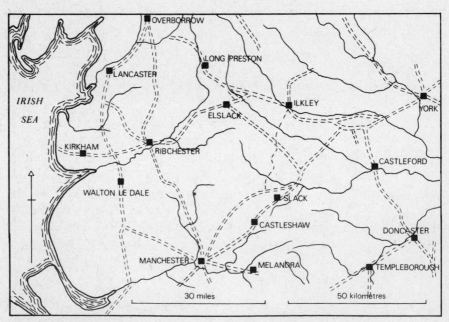

Fig. 20 Roman forts and roads in north-west England

of northern Scotland and the increasing strain on the troops forced it to advance along the east coast, north-east of Stirling towards Aberdeen and even beyond. A single road marks this line.

This rapid conquest of north Britain was a remarkable feat of arms, even by Roman military standards, but it was also an incredible achievement in terms of road engineering. For the troops involved not only had to fight their way over some of the roughest country in Britain, but they also had to build at least sixty fortresses and construct a bare minimum of 1300 miles of roads and probably much more. The campaign by Agricola was the maximum advance of the Roman army; the following years saw its gradual withdrawal from much of Scotland as the military pressures became too great. Eventually the permanent frontier returned to the line of Hadrian's Wall, although the Roman army continued to operate in parts of Scotland until the third century AD.

This then is, in outline, the story of the development of the military roads of Roman Britain. And though their prime purpose was to serve the army, in south-east Britain at least they soon took over a more peaceful role as part of a greater road system connected with the economic development of the country. This brings us to the second class of Roman roads, those which may be called economic ones. In fact the separation of these from the military roads is a false one, for not only were they all probably built by the army, but it is also very difficult to distinguish one type from another. Nevertheless the distinction is worth making, for there were roads in Britain whose purpose was more connected with the commercial exploitation of the country than with its military conquest.

From the very beginning of the Roman occupation, and indeed perhaps before it, the Romans were determined to exploit the wealth of the country. Minerals were a particularly important source of wealth in Britain, and some must have been well known to the conquerors. One of the first areas to be mined, for example, was the Mendip Hills, in Somerset, where the Roman army seems to have started extracting lead on a large scale soon after the initial conquest. The lead had to be transported eastwards to the channel ports and certainly one road seems to have been used – the one which runs south-east from the Mendips across Wiltshire to Salisbury, then on to Winchester and thence to the coast. It does not appear to have a major military role in the conquest of the area, but it was certainly in being by AD 49 for a lead ingot of that date has been found alongside it in Hampshire and two more near Southampton. Another important lead-mining area was in Derbyshire which was certainly being worked in the first century AD. Again, from the evidence of ingots some of the lead at least was sent down the road from Buxton to Doncaster, presumably on its way to the Humber for shipment abroad.

Lead was also worked in Shropshire, Cumbria and Northumberland, though there the exact roads used for its dispatch are unknown. Also unknown are the routes along which the metal was moved from the extensive copper deposits in Anglesey as well as the north Welsh mainland and Shropshire.

More definite evidence is that for the trade in tin from Cornwall. Though at the moment only one major Roman road, and that probably an early military one, is known, running down the spine of the peninsula, the discovery of mid third-century milestones in the country suggests a major road building programme at that time to link up the various tin mines. The discovery of pewter blocks in the Thames at Battersea might perhaps indicate that tin came back across southern England to London, though of course sea-borne trade cannot be discounted. Other major extractive industries included gold in Wales and coal from a variety of sources, though again little is known about the roads used. More important perhaps was the iron industry. The major areas of iron working in Roman Britain were in the Weald of south-east England and in the Forest of Dean. In the former area there seems to have been a deliberate policy of constructing roads to link up with minor tracks serving the mines and furnaces. No less than three major roads run south from London across the Weald to the coast, more than mere military or day-to-day commercial traffic would have needed.

In addition to these products, a whole host of other goods was produced in various places as Roman civilization was imposed on Britain. Among the most important was pottery, manufactured in major industrial complexes in Roman Britain, located in a number of specific places. The wares made there were, in most cases, traded over a fairly limited area, usually up to about fifty miles. Even here roads must often have been busy with pottery merchants and traders. However certain types of pots were sold over much wider areas, those made in the New Forest, Hampshire, for example, were sent all over southern England. Likewise a type of pottery produced in the Oxford area reached places as far away as Richborough in Kent

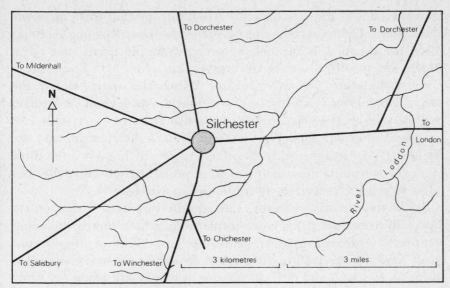

Fig. 21 Roman roads around Silchester

and Caernarvon in north Wales. Even more spectacular are products of the huge pottery manufacturing region in the lower Nene Valley, around Peterborough. The industry there probably started in the early second century and by AD 200 the pottery was reaching all parts of Britain.

The roads of Britain were also used to carry valuable imports, demanded by the Romanized Britons as their standard of living gradually rose. These included wine from France, which certainly reached places such as Silchester near Reading as well as Lincoln and York; fine glazed Samian pottery, also from France, which is found everywhere in Britain, as well as fine metalwork and olive oil. Even rare marble from the Mediterranean was brought in to decorate public buildings and private homes.

All these products, as well as many others, were moved along the main roads of Roman Britain, which became the arteries of the province: its defence, economic growth and political administration could never have been achieved without them. As trade developed and civil administration grew in the years after the conquest, not all the military roads were sufficient. Many were, as the original forts along them grew into towns, but elsewhere new roads were required to link the new towns. It is not easy to distinguish these from the

military roads or the long-distance economic ones but there are some
indications. The important site of Silchester, near Reading in Berkshire, for instance, is the hub of seven radiating roads, not all of
which can possibly be early military roads (Fig. 21). The ones to
London, Salisbury, Cirencester and Winchester may be, but the
two to Dorchester (Oxfordshire), and that to Mildenhall (Wiltshire)
may be seen as later civil routes. Likewise at Cirencester (Gloucestershire), while the Foss Way is certainly a military road, and the
Silchester-Gloucester road is also likely to be one in origin, the three
other roads leading from the town were probably built after the conquest to serve Cirencester, its trade and its citizens.

Below these roads in status, but equally important, were others
especially constructed for more local traffic which linked the small
centres of settlement to their nearest towns. Many of these minor
roads have not survived to the present day; their discovery and identification is a long and difficult process which is still going on. Only
in a few places is anything like the true pattern emerging. One such
area is in the south-east Midlands (Fig. 22), where as a result of the
most detailed searching for clues, the real picture of Roman roads in
southern Britain becomes clear. There is an intricate web of routes,
extending in every direction, so that even the most remote farmstead, or isolated hamlet, was never more than six or seven miles
from a fine well-made road. In a sense this is the real impact of
Roman civilization on the history of roads, more influential perhaps
than the great military roads, or the long-distance trading routes. It
was this complex system of minor roads that really drew Britain into
the Roman Empire and allowed that empire to influence the people
in every possible social, political and economic way.

The total length of all the known Roman roads in Britain is not far
short of 8000 miles. Many known stretches of road end abruptly and,
at the moment, cannot be traced to their certain destination. As a
result we can certainly add at least another 500 miles to the total
and, in addition, many hundreds of miles still await discovery, especially the minor local roads. Thus we will not be far out if we say
that the Romans built not less than 10,000 miles of road between the
first and fourth centuries AD, most of which were probably built in
the first hundred years. This was no mean achievement when one
considers that these roads were constructed over moors and mountains, through marshes and forests, and across wide rivers, deep
ravines and thousands of streams. It is very important to note that

I  Prehistoric trackway and settlement, Tallington, Lincolnshire, showing
as a crop mark

II   Paved Roman road, Wheeldale Moor, North Yorkshire

III   Roman road, Martin Down, Hampshire

IV  Roman trackway running between contemporary fields, Winterbourne
    Houghton, Dorset

V   Dark Age or earlier lane, Gorran, Cornwall

VI   Medieval road from London to Norwich, Cavenham Heath, Suffolk

VII   Medieval and later holloways, Goathland, North Yorkshire

these roads were *constructed*. Every one was specially built, largely by hand, using fairly simple technology. It is at these methods we must now look.

As we have already seen, the main roads of Roman Britain were laid out as part of a carefully thought-out plan during the initial military conquest, for the subsequent period of military control or for long-distance trade and communications. They were thus more like a railway system then any other roads in the history of Britain until the motorways of recent years. And, like a railway system, and indeed the motorways, the main Roman roads were planned by engineers, following detailed ground survey, and were finally constructed by a supremely trained work force. In addition, for the military roads at least, the work had to be carried out on active service, in hostile country and frequently in unsuitable terrain. The later trade or civil roads were probably not so difficult to survey or construct but even so all of them represent a remarkable achievement. Most of the work of road survey and building was in the hands of the

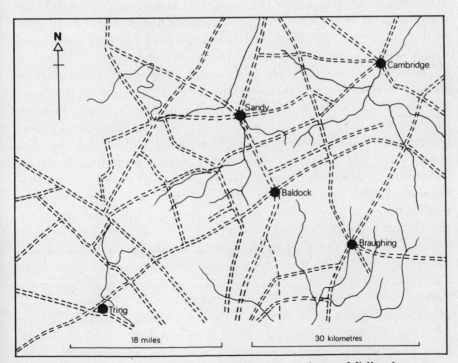

Fig. 22 Major and minor Roman roads in the south-east Midlands

Roman army. This is certainly so in the case of the military roads, and though the civil roads may have been planned and constructed under the orders of either national or local government bodies, the actual work was probably carried out by military engineers, or at least by men trained in army methods.

The most characteristic feature of Roman roads is the straight alignment on which they are laid out. Indeed it is that which so often enables us to identify them today. However, straight alignments are not an invariable characteristic and if the local topography demanded it a Roman road took the easiest or most convenient course. This was particularly true of the upland mountain areas, where roads often followed winding valley bottoms or irregular ridge tops, but it is also often the case where steep valley sides had to be crossed. Here roads were usually turned to give an easier descent. Nevertheless, even in these places, the roads were usually laid out in a series of very short straight lengths rather than on a continuous curve. A fine example of this may be seen on the road from Winchester in Hampshire to the Roman town of Cunetio near Mildenhall in Wiltshire. From Winchester the road runs almost exactly straight for some eighteen miles across rolling chalk downland. Then north-west of Andover, near the village of Chute, the road builders were faced with a deep, steep-sided coombe, running at right angles to the line of the road and presenting them with a very steep descent, followed by an even steeper ascent if they were to continue the road on the existing line (Fig. 23). No doubt if the road had been an early military one, for use mainly by marching troops, the problem would have been ignored and the road driven across the valley. But this was a civil road, not a military one, and it linked the rich agricultural cornlands of Hampshire with the more wealthy and fashionable Gloucestershire Cotswolds. It was therefore a road for wheeled traffic, much of it probably carrying heavy goods, and the steep slopes had to be avoided at all costs. The result was that the road builders diverted the road westwards in a broad arc four-and-a-half miles long, instead of the two-and-a-quarter mile direct route, thus involving only slight gradients. Nevertheless this diversion was not a curve. It was made up of nine short alignments, each between one-quarter and three-quarters of a mile long, which gradually turned the road through almost 180° until it reached the original overall line. Thereafter the road continued across the downs as before.

The main reason for this emphasis on straight lengths was almost certainly because it was the easiest way of carrying out the initial survey. We have no written sources in Britain, nor elsewhere in the Roman Empire, to tell us how the surveys were carried out, but there is a collection of late Roman manuals on land surveying which has come down to us. These show that Roman surveyors were well versed in the principles of map making, land and boundary surveys and thus the laying out of roads would have been no problem for them at all.

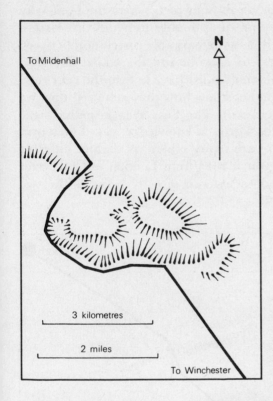

Fig. 23 Roman road, Chute Causeway, Wiltshire

The process of laying out the line of a proposed Roman road would seem to have involved three major stages. The first was what may be called general reconnaissance. One of the most remarkable features, especially of the long lengths of Roman road in southern Britain, is the knowledge of the overall geography of an area that they indicate. Before even the detailed survey work commenced, the road planners knew exactly where they were going, not just in a general sense but often to within a few hundred yards. Today it is relatively easy with accurate maps for a road planner to fix a proposed motorway line from, say, London to Birmingham. But how did the Roman road planners manage the same feat without, as far as we know, any maps at all? The Foss Way, from Axminster in Devon to Lincoln, for example, is just over 200 miles long. It was, as we have already seen, planned, surveyed and laid out in the middle of a military campaign. Yet its actual line never deviates more than about eight miles away from the direct line between these two places. Some of the deviations are the result of having to avoid long stretches of unsuitable terrain, as in Somerset, where the Foss Way lies to the east of the direct line, presumably to avoid the eastern part of the Somerset Levels. But the remarkable correlation between the direct line from Axminster to Lincoln and the actual line is so close that the original road planners must have known the *exact* relationship between them. We do not know how they achieved this; we can only stand in awe of their skill. The Foss Way is perhaps the best example of this stage of background knowledge, based on a firm topographical sense, but there are many others. A slightly different instance is the Stane Street, which runs from London to Chichester (Fig. 24). Though this road does not run directly between the two

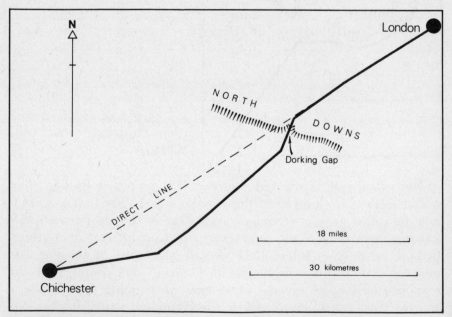

Fig. 24 Roman road from London to Chichester

towns, it is not without significance that the first fifteen miles between London Bridge and Ewell in Surrey points exactly to Chichester. That is, the precise bearing of Chichester from London was
clearly known and the first part of the road was laid out on it. The
subsequent route from Ewell to Chichester deviated considerably
from the initial line by up to six miles but this was due to the sens-
ible use of the Mole Gap near Dorking, where the River Mole cuts
the North Downs, rather than allowing the road to cross the steep
scarp face to the west. Again the overall grasp by the Roman road
engineers of the geography of wide areas in the initial planning
stage is obvious.

Yet in spite of this we must not be blinded by the magnitude of
these achievements into thinking that it was entirely the result of
efficient Roman methods and organization. We must also remember
the landscape and social organization of the people the Roman army
conquered, and in particular the complex and sophisticated pattern of communications that already existed when the Roman army
arrived: the Roman road planners were faced with a highly
developed landscape, with many settlements linked by trackways so,
at the very least, the background geography and the relationships of
places were all well known and rapid movement across the land was
by no means difficult. Thus the Roman road planners, while not
perhaps having actual maps to guide them, must have had an almost
complete picture of the countryside on which they were to impose
their new road system.

Having decided the overall route for their roads, the second stage
of construction must have been a detailed examination of the
ground, to decide the actual line. This presumably involved looking
at the topography of the terrain on either side of the general route, in
order to establish the best places to cross rivers, avoid steep slopes
and skirt unsuitable marshy areas. Again during this phase, the
existing trackways, as well as the knowledge obtainable from the
newly conquered peoples, must have been enormously helpful to this
detailed local planning. It was presumably also at this stage that the
minor deviations of alignments or major changes of direction were
decided upon, as a result of this background knowledge as well as
from the close study of the landscape. In the areas already under
Roman control many of these decisions were no doubt made in order
to obtain the easiest route for subsequent traffic or to avoid totally
unsuitable country; but in the military areas, on the other hand, the

immediate problem of linking forts and laying down routes for infantry patrols as well as for lines of communication and supply must have been the major consideration.

Examples of all these apparent problems and their solutions can be fairly easily recognized whenever Roman roads are looked at carefully. Both the major and minor alterations to the basic planned route of a civil road can be seen on that between Sailsbury in Wiltshire and Badbury in Dorset. By a direct line these two centres are some twenty miles apart and the intervening country is generally rolling chalk downland with few steep slopes. It probably would have seemed at the planning stage of the road that no major deviations were necessary, but close examination of the ground would have immediately revealed a major difficulty. The direct line, though an easy route in general terms, is complicated thirteen miles south-west of Salisbury by an irregularly shaped high area of chalk, capped by clay, known as the Pentridge and Blagdon Hills. This rises to well over 500 feet above OD (Ordnance Datum, i.e. above sea level) and has particularly steep slopes on its south side. For the sake of subsequent traffic, the direct line had to be abandoned and the actual line moved either east or west of the hills. To move it to the east would have meant further problems, including steeper slopes and a long run up the winding marshy valley of the River Allen. To move it west was much better, as this line would be on dry open chalkland for much of the way with relatively gentle slopes across the south-east trending valleys. As far as we can tell, the decision was made to align the road west of the direct route so that it passed to the west of Pentridge Hill, and it was thus given two major changes of alignment to achieve this.

However, having made that decision, another problem had to be faced. Though, as has been noted, most of the chalk valleys that the road had to cross have gentle slopes, just south of Salisbury, for complex geological reasons, the valley of the River Ebble is deep. The north side is a gentle slope but the south side is a steep scarp with a highly indented face, consisting of rounded spurs and deep coombes (Fig. 25). Even the direct line would have had to cross the Ebble Valley so that the final deviation made little difference here and the problem still had to be solved. The chosen alignment of the road from Salisbury ran obliquely down the north side of the Ebble Valley and across the river. To have continued the road on this alignment would have meant climbing a low spur, dropping down into a tributary valley, then climbing another spur, dropping down into the next coombe, and crossing a further spur into yet another coombe, before climbing steeply up to reach the top of the scarp. This unsatisfactory line was, in fact, altered by a small diversion made up of three short alignments. The actual road when it reached the first spur beyond the river was turned some 20° to the south, so that it ran along the crest of the spur following the easiest slope. When it reached the top of the spur it was turned south-west again to run almost parallel with the original alignment until it was clear of the edge of the indented scarp. It was then turned again some 40° along the edge of the scarp until it met the original alignment.

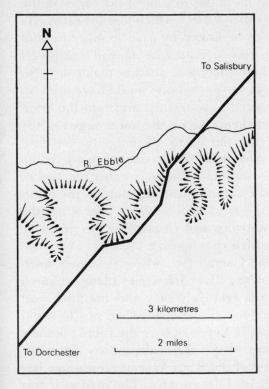

Fig. 25 Roman road,
Ebble Valley, Wiltshire

The same kind of problems had to be faced on the roads in the north and in Wales, though here, as far as we can see, the military needs were paramount. The control of the eastern lowlands of southern Scotland, for instance, was based on the large fort at Newstead, near Melrose. This fort was built in the centre of the land occupied by the tribe known as the Selgovae and just below their fortified tribal capital which the Roman army slighted. Thus military strategy demanded that the main fort be at Newstead, and as a result the main road north across the uplands, known as Dere Street, had to take the most direct route over the often difficult terrain. Very steep gradients had to be accepted, and in many places no definite alignments were possible. The road planners had to pick their way as best they could and in particular they were forced to use a narrow ridgeway between the headwaters of the Hindhope Burn and the River Coquet, exactly on the present England-Scotland border, where a small fort was established.

In Wales the evidence is similar. A fort was built at Llandovery, near the centre of that country, no doubt to control the valley of the River Tywi and the numerous other valleys which join it nearby. As a military centre the fort had to be linked by road to other forts of the defence system. In particular a road had to run north-east towards Llandrindod Wells where there was another major fort. No direct route was possible, though the easiest one would have been up the valley of the Afon Bran, over the watershed and into the Irfon valley to Llanwrtyd Wells, and thence along the lower slopes of the mountain to Llandrindod Wells, the route taken by the modern road, incidentally. However, this option was not taken up in its entirety. For presumably purely military reasons, another fort had to be established at a place called Caerau on the highland to the south of Llanwrtyd Wells and thus the road which had to pass it left the Bran valley north-east of Llandovery and climbed to the ridgeway through the Crychan Forest, which rises to over 1100 feet above OD. It then turned east to reach the Caerau fort, where it turned north and descended to the crossing of the River Irfon near Llangammarch Wells. From here, the route was relatively easy and the final road seems to be made up of three general alignments laid out to avoid the steep sides of the major valley. Yet even here the route planners had a difficult task. The centre of the three alignments, from the village of Beulah to the crossing of the River Wye at Newbridge has to pass through some very difficult hilly country. The road as it was built had to twist and turn to avoid narrow valleys and major hills. Even so a number of gradients up to one in seven had to be constructed.

These examples, and many that could have been chosen, illustrate the amount of detailed planning that, for a variety of reasons, went into Roman roads before construction work began. However, before the road building programme commenced, yet another stage of work had to be carried out – the fixing of the line on the ground by surveyors. The remarkable straightness of long sections of Roman roads and their abrupt turns where new alignments began have often excited the admiration of modern students of these roads. Yet if we assume that all the planning described above was carried out, the surveying was a relatively simple process, demanding no instruments and little skill. In fact this brings us to the real reason why Roman roads are usually straight. It was for the convenience of setting out the actual course by relatively unskilled soldiers as quickly as possible. Once the overall direction of the road was fixed, small groups of men could lay out the actual line using nothing more than a set of movable beacons or markers visible over long distances. The theory behind this is well known to anybody who has done simple surveying. It is that one can arrange a line of poles or markers between two points, merely by looking along the line between the two points and then moving intermediate markers alternately to the left or to the right until all are in a straight line. So if the decision has been made to carry a road across the countryside from point *A* to point *B*, as long as point *B* is visible from point *A* a straight line can be laid across the intervening land, no matter how broken by hills or valleys it may be, and even if in many places on that line neither *A* no *B* is visible. The method of work is illustrated in Fig. 26. If *A* and *B* are the ends of the alignment of the road, easily visible markers are positioned on these points. Then, by placing similar markers on the intervening points *C* and *D*, and moving them about, a straight line of sight can be established from *A* through *C* and *D* to *B*. It is then possible to put in another set of markers at *A1* and *A2* and fix the line of sight in the valley between *A* and *C*. Likewise, by placing

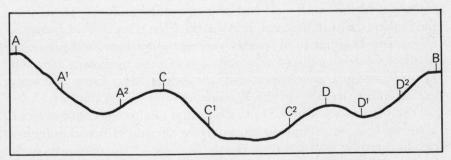

Fig. 26 Diagram to illustrate the laying out of a Roman road

similar markers between *C* and *D* (*C1* and *C2* or more if necessary) and in the valley between *D* and *B* (*D1* and *D2*), the exactly straight alignment can be fixed quite simply and quickly.

We do not know what types of markers were used. Over some of the very long alignments, which may have been as much as ten to fifteen miles apart, it is probable that even large markers would have been invisible and that perhaps fires in baskets, probably at night, were used to establish the overall runs. On shorter alignments, and particularly for the intermediate points, large 'target' markers, or even stout poles, as long as they were easily manoeuvrable, were no doubt used. The main requirement of this method was that the places where the overall alignments changed direction needed to be clearly visible from their adjacent points. Usually this is said to result in the use of high ridges or prominent hills, and this explains why Roman roads do usually change direction most frequently at such places. However, while it is true that high points were used in this way, if we examine many stretches of Roman roads with care, we can see that this is not entirely so and that other factors played a major part in the decisions as to where the main changes of alignment were made. A good example of this is the Watling Street (now the A5) running across the south-east Midlands from the Roman town at Magiovinium, just outside Bletchley in Buckinghamshire to High Cross in Leicestershire. A major change of alignment occurs just south-east of Magiovinium, at the modern village of Little Brickhill on the summit of a high ridge. The road then runs north-west in an exactly straight line for nearly eight miles, first down a steep hill, then through Magiovinium itself, across the River Ousel and then over rather rolling country crossing the seven small valleys of north-east flowing streams. Just before the modern town of Stony Stratford, the alignment abruptly changes to the north. The point of change is at the south-west end of a low ridge and, though it is not the highest point in the area, it is visible from the previous change of alignment. It seems to be merely the best place hereabouts from the point of view of visibility at which to make the necessary turn. The next alignment is nine miles long, across the River Ouse and again across rolling country to the Roman town of Towcester, which lies on the edge of the River Tove, where the alignment changes again. Here we have an interesting situation for the end of this alignment is not intervisible with the first, partly because of the distance, partly because of the numerous ridges across the axis of the road, but mainly because of the steep slopes on the south side of the Tove Valley south of Towcester. As Towcester was probably an existing fort when the road was being constructed, both points were known, so the actual alignment must have been laid out by a slightly different method from that indicated earlier. In this case lines of sight must have been laid out simultaneously from each end of the alignment approximately in the desired direction. When the two lines of markers met they would then have been moved from side to side until the whole line was straight (Fig. 27). This would seem to be a laborious task, but if the pre-planning stage had been thorough and the geography of the area well understood, the first projected line would have been close to the desired line.

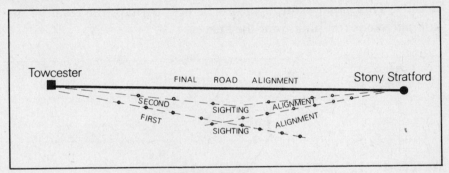

Fig. 27 Diagram to illustrate the laying out of a Roman road

At Towcester the alignment changes again and begins a long, almost straight run of nearly fifteen miles terminating on a high flat-topped hill between the villages of Kilsby and Crick in Northamptonshire. Again this point and Towcester are not intervisible; presumably the method outlined above was used to fix this alignment. However the alignment is not exactly straight and there are at least two minor bends in it, so slight as to be almost unrecognizable, one near Weedon Bec and the other near the next Roman town Bannaventa, near Whilton. These very minor changes in line are not uncommon on Roman roads. Thirty have been noted on the road between Canterbury and Rochester in Kent, for example. They have been, probably correctly, explained as either indicating the degree of latitude allowed in the siting of the major long-distance alignments, or the result of chance conditions of long-distance visibility on the day that the sighting was done, or both. While this explanation may also be true on the Watling Street in Northamptonshire, there were additional problems on this road which may have contributed to the slight misalignments.

Eight miles out from Towcester, at Weedon Bec, the road had to cross the River Nene, here only a minor stream but flowing in a broad marshy valley at the point where one of its tributaries from the north joins it. If the major alignment had been followed the subsequent road would have had not only to cross the Nene but also the tributary stream four times, all in less than a mile. To avoid this the road was carried round the winding tributary by means of three short alignments to the west until the main alignment was regained (Fig. 28). This was an eminently practical solution to the problem, but at the end of the diversion the main alignment was not followed exactly. This minor error, if such it be, was perhaps the result of the complications resulting from the survey.

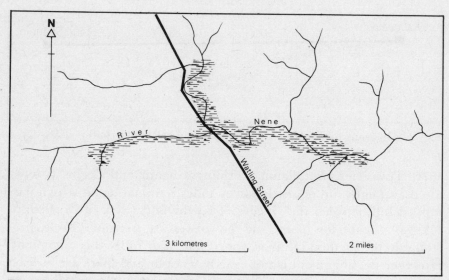

Fig. 28 Roman road, Weedon Bec, Northamptonshire

At the end of this alignment near Kilsby a new one begins. Here it was clearly intended to run direct to the next major change at High Cross in Leicestershire where the Foss Way, running south-west from Leicester, crossed the Watling Street. However this alignment is again a long one, of some thirteen miles. In addition, though both ends are on high ground, and are this time intervisible, because the intervening ground is very broken by the valleys of numerous small streams as well as that of the River Avon, the alignment has two minor changes in its length. These are both towards the north, where the deep valley of the River Swift and the generally flat plateau land to the north of it seem to have led to some survey errors. These changes were presumably within the agreed latitude allowed to the surveyors.

So far we have looked at the pre-planning, planning and surveying stages of Roman road design. We have now reached the point in the process where the final line of a road would have been marked by the series of posts or beacons across the countryside that the actual road builders could follow. However, it may be that there was yet another stage after this, before the road construction gangs moved in.

As we shall see in Chapter 5, in the late eighteenth and early nineteenth centuries similar straight roads were constructed over Britain, though for a very different purpose. At that time, though the main alignments of these roads were fixed by poles or markers, in many places, to allow the actual road builders to follow it more easily, a single furrow was ploughed along its line between markers. We have no proof that this technique was ever used in Roman Britain, but this method, using a plough furrow to mark out land settlements, roads and even future towns, is well documented in classical literature. When the poet Virgil gives a picture of Aeneas founding a city in Sicily, for example, he uses the words: 'interea Aeneas urbem designat aratro sortiturque domos' (meanwhile Aeneas marks the city out by ploughing; then he draws the homes by lot). Likewise Statis, telling us about the preparatory work involved in the Emperor Domitian's new road to Naples, says that the line of the road had to be marked out with furrows.

It is likely, therefore, that the lines of many Roman roads were finally fixed *on the ground* either by plough furrows, or possibly by shallow ditches, to mark the centre line of the road to be. Such furrows or ditches ought to have been recognized by archaeologists excavating Roman roads, though it seems that they have not in most cases. On the other hand, it may be that the archaeologists have not looked for the very slight traces that may exist. There is one possible example of this: a section cut across the Salisbury-Badbury Rings Roman road, on the Dorset-Hampshire border, showed a shallow ditch of markedly asymmetrical profile, filled with loamy soil, cut into the ground surface near the cente of the later road and sealed by the constructed road itself. This may have been the marking out ditch or furrow of the pre-constructional phase.

Up to now we have been looking at the way the major military and civil roads were planned and surveyed. These are the ones that are the most obvious in the present landscape, but the minor civil roads also need to be examined for in some respects they differ from the major ones in a number of important details, especially with regard to planning and surveying. As we have already seen, the majority of these minor roads were laid out after the main ones and usually covered relatively short distances, linking the smaller towns and minor settlements. They were thus planned and laid out with different concepts in mind, to different standards, and probably by less skilled engineers than the major roads. As a result, though the same principles of planning and surveying were used, there was not the same rigid adherence to long straight alignments, and short lengths were employed to fit even minor irregularities on the ground. A good example of this kind of road may be seen near Peterborough. Around the village of Castor, in the centre of a major pottery making area, at least four major roads meet the main Ermine Street. One of these roads leaves the Ermine Street and runs north-east towards Peterborough. From it a minor road only one mile long extends south-east into a deep bend of the River Nene, heading towards the site of a wharf on the river (Fig. 29). Apart from a gentle slope down the valley side, this road runs on almost flat ground for most of its length. Yet in spite of this it goes through a most extraordinary series of sharp changes of alignment and even ends on a broad curve in a most un-Roman manner. There is no obvious explanation for such a layout, and one can only conclude that the normal rules of roads were largely ignored here by those who designed it, perhaps because they regarded them as unnecessary. It is also possible that the builders were incorporating their road into a pre-existing system of boundaries which could not be ignored. Usually the major Roman roads of Britain totally disregarded man-made features.

Another type of road where the usual methods were at least partly waived was what may be called the Romanized trackways, that is, the apparent improvement of some of the older long-distance trackways which were discussed in the last chapter. There is a purely technical problem here in that, because of the complications mentioned earlier in the dating of these trackways and then disentangling

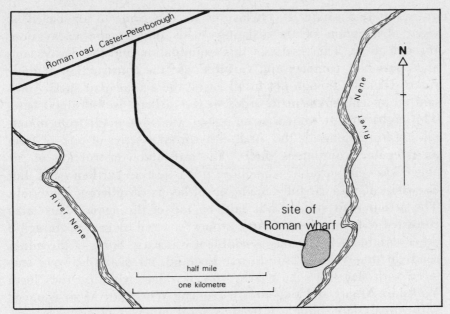

Fig. 29 Roman road, Castor, Cambridgeshire

the later usage of parts of them, it is very difficult now to see which sections were altered or improved by the Romans. Along the line of the so-called Icknield Way in east Hertfordshire and south-east Cambridgeshire, for example, is a series of almost straight green lanes, known as Ashwell Street. These have often been called a Roman road, yet in fact it has been proved beyond doubt that the exactly straight alignments are the result of laying out new drove roads in the nineteenth century and thus a Roman origin is extremely doubtful. However, elsewhere there is evidence that the general line of an existing trackway was followed, even if it was in a different place. Such a situation can be seen also on the Icknield Way, further south-east in Buckinghamshire and Oxfordshire. There, what is normally said to be the prehistoric Icknield Way runs along the crest of the north-facing Chiltern scarp (Fig. 30). Below it, at the foot of the scarp, is another road which can be traced from near Wendover, for some sixteen miles, to Watlington, and though it is by no means straight or on true alignments, it is likely to be of Roman date.

So at last we come to the final stage in the making of Roman roads, the actual construction. Once again we have no written evidence to go on, and so whatever conclusions we can come to are based on close observation of the existing roads and of the excavations through them. The results of this examination and the excavations show just how complex and variable was the construction of these roads. Usually, though not in all cases, the actual road surface was laid on an embankment in order to give a firm, well-drained base. This embankment, known as an agger, was often made from material dug from alongside the road, either from a series of pits, or from an irregular, continuous ditch. The size and construction of the agger was very variable: sometimes it was just an earthen bank, but elsewhere it was carefully made up of layers of different materials. The actual road surface was laid on top of the agger. This often consisted of foundations of large stones, covered by gravel, though if other suitable material was available it was used. Some of the minor roads in the Weald of south-east England, for example, were surfaced with slag from the nearby iron working, while on the North Yorkshire Moors, the long stretch crossing Wheeldale Moor is paved with stone slabs obtained from a local outcrop of suitable rock (Plate II).

However, these points are little more than generalizations. If we look in detail at a road which has been examined in a number of places we will see that the actual structure of the road could and did vary greatly. The Roman road between Salisbury and Dorchester, for example, has been excavated in at least five places. On the section between Salisbury and Badbury three sections have been examined, all within a distance of two miles. Here the road consists of a fine, raised embankment, running across dry chalkland (Plate III). In the first section at Woodyates, close to the Dorset-Hampshire county boundary, the agger was made by spreading a layer of large flints on the ground surface, and covering these with a large bank of rammed chalk. The road surface itself, a layer of gravel obtained from Pentridge Hill, one-and-a-half miles to the south-east, had been laid on top of this chalk bank. Another section cut through the road, only a quarter of a mile further north at Bokerley Dyke, revealed a slightly different structure. At the bottom were the same flint nodules with a thin bed of rammed chalk over it. On top was a thick layer of gravel, also obtained from Pentridge Hill, but the road surface here was of chalk. The third section was cut across the road one-and-a-half miles south of the first and was different again. Though there was a base of flint as before, the whole agger was

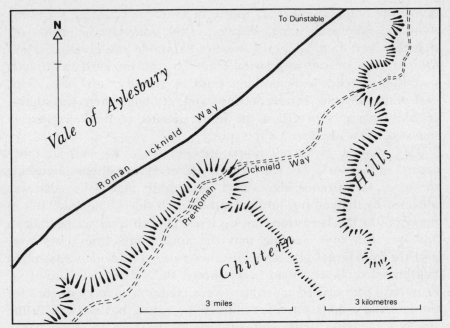

Fig. 30 Roman and prehistoric Icknield Way, Chiltern Hills

made out of successive layers of chalk, gravel and earth, often mixed up and clearly showing less care of construction than in the other two places.

The same road has also been examined sixteen miles further south-west, near the village of Winterbourne Kingston on its way from Badbury to Dorchester. Here again it is still on chalk downland, but the agger is different. A bed of clay had been laid on the ground surface and this was covered by a thin band of flints and small stones which was the actual road surface itself. To the south-west again, just before the road reached Dorchester, at a point where it is crossing an area of gravel and sandy heathland, a further excavation showed that the agger was merely gravel laid directly on the original ground surface.

This evidence from a single Roman road is of considerable interest, for it tells us much about how such a road was constructed, not merely in the harsh technical terms of the materials used but, if we think about it, in the manner in which the workmen involved went about their tasks. For it is clear that there was considerable flexibility in the rules of making a road such as this which, after all, was one of the major commercial routes of southern England. Certainly there was no overall standardization in the materials, or in the way that they were laid; whatever was most suitable and obtainable was utilized. The overall impression from excavations such as these is that Roman roads were perhaps built by small groups of soldiers, each responsible for certain sections and, although there was almost certainly overall supervision, the actual detailed method of construction was left to the men on the spot.

This view is given additional support when we look at other aspects of the work. The existence of pits or quarry ditches alongside the agger, for instance, shows that much of the material needed was obtained by digging it from the land on each side of the road. But in many places the roads have no evidence of such quarries near them and one can only assume that the spoil came from elsewhere, perhaps from larger pits, some distance away. The evidence from the Salisbury-Dorchester road also shows this. The excavations at Bokerley Dyke proved that there were continual quarry ditches for the necessary chalk on either side of the agger, but set well to the side of it. Further south-west, near Badbury, there are outer banks beyond the side ditches which still survive, but at the point near Dorchester where it was examined no ditches or pits of any kind were discovered. Here again it appears that individual working parties were left to decide the details of the construction themselves.

The width of Roman roads was also very variable. Basically the agger, where built, was much wider than the surfaced road. On the important cross-country civil and military roads of southern Britain, the actual roads are between twenty and thirty feet wide though the aggers can be twice that. Again, where well-preserved stretches of Roman road survive undamaged, the width and indeed the height of the aggers can vary over relatively short distances. Thus where Ermine Street, the main road from London to the north, leaves the Roman town of Durobrivae, to the west of Peterborough it runs on a large agger some thirty feet across and three feet high. But after two or three miles it increases to almost forty feet across though only two feet high. A few miles to the north again, after crossing the River Welland near Stamford, it is still nearly six feet high, even after modern ploughing has much reduced it. On the smaller local roads, or on the military roads in difficult country, the width of the agger is often less than twenty feet and sometimes as little as ten to twelve feet.

Sometimes the aggers are of such a size as to question their necessity. Again the Salisbury-Dorchester road shows this well. Where it crosses the north Dorset downland the actual road is on a massive agger forty to fifty feet wide and four to six feet high (Plate III). Such a height seems totally unnecessary on well-drained downland. It has often been suggested that, as this road was passing through a district exceptionally well populated by native Britons, the agger was meant to impress on them The Might of Rome. However this does not seem to be a particularly convincing explanation, especially when we now know that there were probably fewer Britons living there than in many other places in the country. This feature only goes to show how little we do know about the aims and attitudes of the builders of these great roads. In this particular case one wonders to what extent rigid military discipline and standards overcome the practical necessities of the road construction.

So far in this examination of the structures of Roman roads we have concentrated almost exclusively on those in the lowland areas of Britain. In the uplands, where most of the roads were for military purposes, both the topography and the military needs produced roads of a different form. The nature of the country itself often precluded the building of great aggers of complex construction, while the hard rocks often prevented the digging of side ditches. In addition many of the roads were not intended for large-scale civilian traffic, but were for military patrols and supply trains, both of which must have been prepared to put up with less sophisticated roadwork.

One of the best examples of this type of military road is that in the Lake District which runs from Ambleside to Ravenglass over the Wrynose and Hard Knott passes. From Ambleside to the head of Little Langdale the course of the road is over easy country. Then at Fell Foot, at about 500 feet above OD, the climb begins. The road leaves the more obvious and easy route along the marshy valley bottom of the River Brathay and runs across the lower slopes of Blake Rigg, as a terrace only four feet wide. It then crosses the Wrynose Beck and curves south-west as a narrow agger some eighteen feet wide. At the summit of Wrynose Pass at 1281 feet above OD the road is lost in marshland, but to the south-west it reappears and starts to run down the valley of the River Duddon, first as a terrace twenty feet wide and then, after crossing the river, as a low causeway up to twenty-four feet across with well-marked curb stones on each side. In the bottom of the valley it recrosses the river, here 700 feet above OD, and then begins the climb over Hard Knott Pass. On the lower slopes it runs on a roughly straight agger twenty feet wide, but as the main fellside is reached, it climbs upwards in a series of zigzags to reach the summit of the pass at 1280 feet above OD. From here the road starts to run down into Eskdale. In order to cross the rocky spur of Raven Crag, a cutting fifteen feet deep and fifteen feet wide at the base was driven through the crag. Beyond the road crosses an area of bare rock, where no structure or surface was possible, and then becomes a prominent agger fifteen feet wide descending in zigzags. At this point, on the hill spur to the north stands Hard Knott Fort, the centre of the Roman military garrison for this area. Two branch roads leave the main one to climb up the fellside and enter the south and west gates of the fort. Beyond the fort, the main road continues down to Eskdale on a terrace fifteen to twenty feet wide, made in another series of zigzags until it reaches the valley bottom, here about 300 feet above OD.

Thus this remarkable road has in the space of five miles, as the crow flies, actually covered about seven miles of some of the roughest country in Britain and twice climbed to over 1200 feet above sea level. It can hardly be considered a well-constructed road, as Roman roads go, but it shows a remarkable adaptation to the physical topography with cuttings, terraces, curves and straight alignments, all built to reduce to a minimum the considerable problems for road users.

The use of terraces and zigzags to overcome the difficulties imposed by steep slopes is not confined to the upland military roads. They were widely used to ease the gradient on all Roman roads that had to cross rapidly rising ground. Indeed, as the steep hills involved have often remained unused since Roman times, it is these terraces that are among the best-preserved parts of Roman roads in Britain. They can often be recognized by their easy and continuous grading, unlike many later medieval trackways, on similar slopes, which wander about in a completely unplanned form. A fine example of one of these terraces can be seen in Gloucestershire, where the so-called Akeman Street from Alcester to Cirencester crosses the valley of the River Leach a little north of the village of Eastleach. The road is running exactly straight towards Circencester, when it meets the deep valley. At the valley edge the road turns sharply and runs down the valley side obliquely as a well-marked terrace ten feet wide. It then crosses the valley bottom on an agger and climbs up the further side on another terrace until, at the crest, it returns to the original

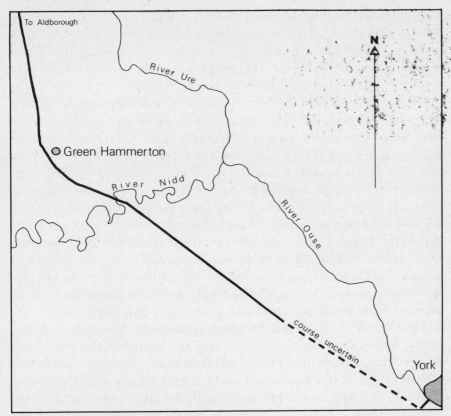

Fig. 31 Roman road from York to Aldborough

alignment and continues south-westwards.

Before completing this examination of the main Roman roads in Britain, we must briefly look at another important aspect of them, the way in which they cross minor and major water courses. Roman roads were, by their very purpose and construction, meant to be all-weather roads, capable of carrying all types of traffic in the easiest and most suitable way, so they had to provide the traveller with reasonably safe methods of crossing water obstacles. There are at least five ways of crossing rivers and streams that the Roman engineers used. The simplest and apparently the most common was the ford. However, there were two problems with fords which the Roman engineers must have had to face. One was that the most suitable natural fords across rivers did not coincide with the alignments or directions of the approach roads which had probably been planned to overcome other difficulties. The other was that natural fords, especially in the lowland rivers, were not always a permanent feature and could in fact move upstream or downstream as a result of floods. Sometimes when the other problems were negligible, it was possible to alter the whole alignment of a road in order to cross a river at a suitable point. This certainly seems to be the case with the main Roman road north from York towards Aldborough (Fig. 31). The obvious route for this road, on leaving York, would seem to have been directly north-west parallel to the River Ouse and its upper reaches called the River Ure. However, it actually leaves York in a west-north-west direction but then, after some nine miles, turns in a series of short alignments to the north-west at the village of Green Hammerton. In effect the actual course of the road followed the two sides of a rather flat triangle instead of the more direct route across the base. The reason for this major deviation is almost certainly because of the River Nidd, which meanders its way north-east to join the Ouse. Though we cannot be certain, it is probable that the road was turned to cross the Nidd two miles upstream from its junction with the Ouse, at a more convenient crossing place.

This example of a major diversion is unusual, however, and normally, unless the river was a large one, the engineers did one of two things. They either turned the road off its main alignment just before it reached the water's edge and carried it to a more suitable fording place or, and apparently far more often, actually built a ford on the original alignment. Nevertheless it is extremely difficult to find these deliberately constructed fords, for the changes wrought by both nature and man on rivers in the last 1800 years have removed most of the evidence. One constructed ford, though now sadly destroyed, was seen many years ago on the road between Rochester and Hastings, at a point near Iden Green, not far from Benenden in Kent. Here the road crossed a small stream and modern downcutting had exposed a well-constructed ford made up of a pavement of roughly squared blocks of stone. These blocks were up to as much as one-and-a-half feet by two feet and seven inches thick. A similar paved ford was found in 1886 on the crossing of the River Tees at Barnard Castle in Durham. The main Roman road here is on the same alignment on each side of the river and, as there was presumably no suitable natural ford, the road plunges straight down the steep valley side and crosses the Tees with no change of alignment at all. In excavations close to the present river the line of the road was marked by an area paved with stone slabs fifteen inches square. Though it is not absolutely certain, it seems likely that these slabs too were part of a deliberately constructed ford.

Where fords were not constructed, did not exist, or the stream to be crossed was narrow but deep, very often a small culvert was built to carry water beneath the road. Once again, as a result of later events, these culverts rarely survive for modern archaeologists to find but in spite of this a number have come to light at various times. One was discovered on the Foss Way between Bath and Cirencester, near the village of Grittleton, where the road crosses a narrow stream. A large flat stone, four feet square, exposed by the recent downcutting of the stream, appears to be the cover stone of a small culvert still in its original position. Where the water courses were wide, or where they were cut so deeply into the underlying rock that fords or culverts were impossible to construct, the normal practice was to build a bridge. A number of Roman bridges are known and the sites of many more can be identified because their earthen abutments, or approach causeways, still survive.

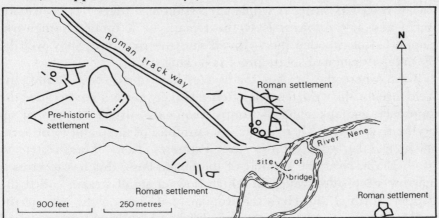

Fig. 32 Roman trackway, Oundle, Northamptonshire

Presumably during the initial stages of the Roman conquest all bridges were of timber. As time went on some of these bridges, especially on the major roads, were rebuilt in stone, although those on less important roads apparently remained of wood throughout the Roman period, even if they had to be rebuilt on numerous occasions. Again the details of the bridges are sparse, but what evidence there is shows that they were often of massive construction. One example was found in 1961 in Northamptonshire where the Godmanchester to Leicester road crossed the River Nene just north of Thrapston.

There gravel quarrying revealed the huge timbers of one side of a large bridge spanning a river which was probably at least thirty yards wide in those days. Modern deepening and widening of major rivers have often removed the traces which were visible to earlier antiquaries. Thus on the Lincoln to London road, the Ermine Street, where it crosses the River Nene just west of Peterborough in Cambridgeshire, there can be no doubt that the Romans built a bridge. Although nothing can be seen today, in the early eighteenth century William Stukeley saw its stone and timber remains at the crossing, and traces of bridges have often been found at the point where a Roman road crosses a major river. Unless one can be sure that later people never built a bridge there, however, we cannot say with certainty that the remains are Roman, for dating is extremely difficult. The Roman road running south-west from Exeter crossed the River Teign at Teignbridge, Devon – but because of tidal water, marshy ground and the existence of other tributary streams there is only one good place to cross the river, that chosen by the Romans and used by all travellers since. A whole succession of bridges has been built there and at the lowest level the remains of a timber framework, supported on wooden piers driven into the river bed, may well be Roman, although absolute proof is lacking.

Even where the bridges themselves have never been found, the evidence for their existence is often relatively easy to see because the approach embankments or ramps frequently survive, extending up to the river edges. There are many examples of these still to be seen, such as the road across the Pennines from Manchester to Rotherham. Near the summit of the Snake Pass, this has to cross a narrow steep-sided valley in which flows a small stream called the Upper North Grain. Here the Roman road ends on the edge of the valley at a large embankment and clearly a high-level bridge carried the road onwards across the stream.

One of the best places to see a succession of the remains of Roman bridges is in County Durham, between Bishop Auckland and Lanchester, where the great military road Dere Street runs north in a series of short alignments across a number of deep valleys of east-flowing streams and rivers. Here one can see the Roman engineers' problems very well indeed, for though such a road had to be passable at all times, the nature of the terrain made this extremely difficult to achieve. Fords were not possible for they would have been dangerous or unusable at frequent times when these streams were in flood. Equally, because of the steep-sided valleys or gills hereabouts, a zigzag terraceway down their sides would have been awkward for heavy wheeled traffic. As a result bridges had to be constructed over all the major streams.

Dere Street leaves the Roman fort at Binchester, just to the north of Bishop Auckland and almost immediately has to cross the wide River Wear. Here, when the river is very low in times of drought, a line of carefully squared blocks of stone is visible in the river bed. In the adjacent banks a number of stones decorated with rusticated panels have been found. It looks from these as if the river was crossed here by a stone bridge of some architectural pretention, supported on three or four piers. Then a quarter of a mile north-west of the River Wear crossing, the road bridges Hunwick Gill (Fig. 33). This is only fifty feet wide but almost twenty-five feet deep. It is therefore too steep and narrow to be negotiated by a zigzag and in any case the agger of the road, here a large sloping ramp, runs to the very edge of the gill and even projects into it. The only interpretation is that a wooden bridge, estimated by D. P. Dymond who discovered the site as probably eleven feet wide, crossed the valley at this point. Twice in the next mile similar valleys are crossed, but as the Roman road is covered by the modern road here the remains of the Roman bridges have not survived. A little further to the north the Roman road crossed another narrow gill, again fifty feet wide and twenty feet deep, called Willington South Dene. As at Hunwick, the road on each side leads right to the edge of the gill. No embankments or abutments were needed, because the road is so high above the

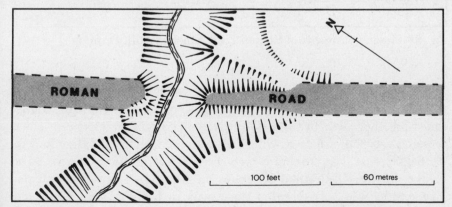

Fig. 33 Bridge abutments of Roman road, Hunwick Gill, Durham

stream, and presumably a timber bridge carried it straight across. Beyond this point two other gills have to be negotiated but, due to modern disturbance, no traces of the undoubted bridges can now be seen. However a little further on the road crosses Stockley Gill (Fig. 34). This is a major valley with a wide flat bottom so here the road was carried down into it, almost to the level of the stream. On both sides, the road ran up to the stream on a large ramp or causeway which slopes abruptly at the edges of the stream to form abutments eight or nine feet high leaving a sixty foot gap to be bridged. Here, within a distance of no more than four-and-a-half miles, the Roman road engineers had to bridge one major river, a considerable stream and six steep-sided valleys, all involving major earthworks, large timber constructions or, in the case of the River Wear, a substantial stone bridge. In this small area we see as well as anywhere the difficulties and final achievements of the great engineers who planned and built our first road system.

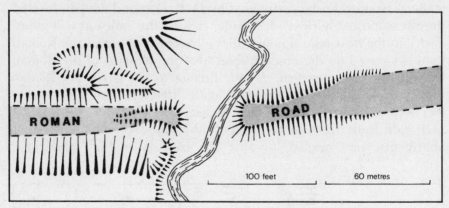

Fig. 34 Bridge abutments of Roman road, Stockley Gill, Durham

In addition to relatively straightforward bridges, the Roman engineers were often forced to build other types of structures, sometimes together with bridges. One particularly difficult type of river crossing was that where a wide, flat-bottomed, marshy valley had to be negotiated. The stream or river itself could be spanned by a bridge, but the ill-drained stretches on either side posed problems. The easiest way to overcome these was to build a long approach causeway, often of considerable height, to carry the traffic well above

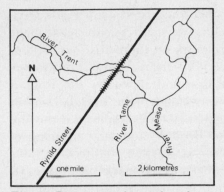

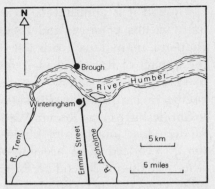

Fig. 35 Roman road crossing the
River Trent, Staffordshire

Fig. 36 Roman road, River
Humber

soft and particularly floodable land. This sometimes had to be stabil-
ized by driving timber piles into the sides of the embankment or by
dumping extra material along it. One place where this kind of
embankment was constructed is on the Winchester to Salisbury road
where it crossed the wide and wet valley of the River Test south of
Stockbridge, Hampshire. There the Roman road can be seen running on top of a large ridge, well above the floodplain of the river. A
better example, though obscured by the modern road which follows
the line, is that of the Ryknild Street between Lichfield and Burton
upon Trent in Staffordshire, where it crosses the almost mile-wide
valley of the River Trent north of Alrewas (Fig. 35). There again the
road is on an embankment three to four feet above the floodplain. In
addition, because the river has and probably always had a considerable number of separate channels, the Roman road must have been
carried, as the modern road is, across a line of separate bridges and
culverts.

Finally it must be noted that sometimes water obstacles were too
much even for the Roman engineers to cope with. Two such places
stand out. One is the crossing of the Severn Estuary between Caerleon on the Welsh side and Sea Mills near Bristol; the other is the
crossing of the Humber between Winteringham and Brough
(Fig. 36). At both of these places a ferry service must have operated
to carry traffic across the estuaries. It is not without significance that
neither of these crossings was bridged until this century when the
Severn Bridge, and the Humber Bridge which is still under construction, show a major technological advance in this respect.

Though it is almost 1600 years since the last Roman roads were built in this country, and though, as we shall see in subsequent chapters, many later roads left their mark on the British landscape, the impact of Roman roads remains very clear. Many of our major trunk routes still follow the exact line laid down by the Roman engineers centuries ago: almost the entire length of the A5 from London to Shrewsbury is the Roman Watling Street, for example, as is the fine modern road north from Lincoln to Brough, and long stretches of the A1. Indeed there are few places, at least in southern Britain, where we do not depend on Roman roads to a remarkable degree. In other ways too they still play an important role in our environment, and some of the main streets of our older towns are basically Roman. Again on the A5, Watling Street, the high streets of places such as Dunstable, Stony Stratford, Towcester and Atherstone are all Roman roads while even at a place as unprepossessing as Burton upon Trent, at least part of the modern town plan is based on the line of the old Roman Ryknild Street. Thus Roman roads are still all around us, not only fulfilling their original purpose as major routes, but also helping to mould the very shapes of parts of our towns.

Yet Roman roads have other functions too in the twentieth century, totally undreamed of by their builders. South Cambridgeshire today is an area of largely arable land and sadly lacks any large open spaces which can be used by the growing population for recreational purposes. One of the few, and certainly one of the most popular places for the citizens of Cambridge to walk along on Sunday afternoons is the Roman road south-east of the town, where there are still some ten miles of an almost straight green lane or bridle path, crossed regularly by later roads which give easy access to it. It now functions as an important place of recreation for thousands of people who obtain great pleasure from its existence; without it we should be socially and aesthetically the poorer.

So far in this chapter we have been solely concerned with the deliberately planned and engineered roads of Roman Britain, but these were not the only lines of communication at this time, or even the most common. For, as well as the roads we usually call Roman, there was a multitude of unplanned trackways and lanes which reached into every corner of Roman Britain and which provided the basic framework for the local, agricultural and social communications pattern.

To understand the background to these tracks, we must remind ourselves of what was said in the previous chapter concerning late prehistoric trackways. There we saw how, in the centuries immediately prior to the Roman invasion, Britain was dotted with farmsteads, each surrounded by extensive fields and linked together by thousands of miles of trackways. The coming of Roman civilization and the establishment of the major roads in Britain did not mean the end of this system of local tracks. Indeed, the reverse is true, and many more thousands of miles of new trackways now appeared, as more farmsteads, villas and even hamlets and villages grew up. The Imperial Peace which the Roman army brought to Britain ended the inter-tribal wars of Iron Age times and allowed people to direct their energies to farming and commerce. More important, as Britain was drawn into the complex economic system of the Roman Empire, the production of a surplus of agricultural products was actively encouraged by the administration, not only to provide supplies for the army which protected the frontiers of Roman Britain, but also to enable an important export trade to be developed. New land was taken into cultivation, more food was produced, wealth and standards of living increased and, inevitably, population rose rapidly.

Some of the increased population was moved or drifted into the large number of new Roman towns which were set up all over the country. These in turn created a new demand for food and a need to take in more land for agricultural purposes. More farms and villages appeared everywhere and vast areas of land were now taken into cultivation and settled for the first time. These areas included not just the ones traditionally thought to have been exploited in the Roman period, such as the Chilterns, Wessex or the limestone plateaux of the Cotswolds, but the heavy claylands of the English Midlands, the lower slopes of the uplands of Wales and northern England, and even the silt fenlands of north Cambridgeshire and south-east Lincolnshire were all developed for agriculture as well. The great medieval forests, such as Wychwood in Oxfordshire, Needwood in Staffordshire and Rockingham Forest in Northamptonshire, were in Roman times largely occupied by fields and pastures, and dotted by small farmsteads and hamlets.

It is difficult for the non-specialist to realize how heavily exploited Britain was at this time, or how dense the rural settlement pattern really was, for archaeologists have tended to hide the information they have recovered in recent years in their own academic journals and books. Yet the picture if looked at carefully is quite surprising.

It has been estimated that in Northamptonshire in Roman times, for example, there were four small farmsteads or hamlets in every square mile, regardless of the type of soil, slope of ground or availability of water. In the fenlands of eastern England, at least in the early Roman period, the density of settlement was, if anything, greater. Even in an upland area such as north Wales, on the lower mountain slopes between 700 feet and 1000 feet above OD, Romanized farm-steads lie little more than a mile apart. In the north the same pattern of dense rural settlement is visible: in a small area south of Penrith in Cumbria on the north-eastern edge of the Lake District, for instance, thirteen Roman settlements have been discovered in an area covering about fifteen square miles. That is nearly one settle-ment every square mile, and we can be sure that many more sites await discovery.

These examples give some idea of the number of settlements and the extent of the agricultural land in use in Roman times. And from the point of view of this book we have to realize that these settle-ments were linked to their fields, to each other, to the main roads and to the towns by a complex system of trackways. The great

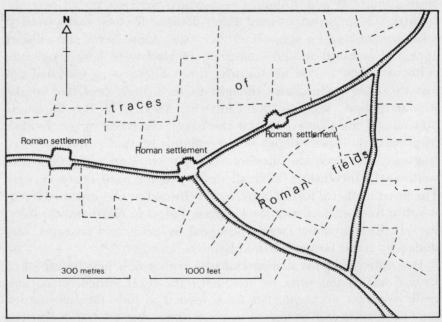

Fig. 37 Roman settlements and tracks, Maiden Newton, Dorset

majority of these trackways either no longer exist because they have been destroyed by later activities, or are still used today as country lanes and thus are not recognized as Roman trackways at all. Where these trackways lay on light soils which produce marks in modern crops they can often be seen from the air today, but most lay on heavy land and no trace is visible now, though the presence of the villas and farmsteads on this type of land show that similar tracks must once have existed there. Air photography has produced some remarkable evidence of Roman trackways which can no longer be seen on the ground today. An example of this appears on both sides of the River Nene, north of Oundle, Northamptonshire (Fig. 32). There a trackway, visible as two parallel marks in the crops, caused by the ditches marking the sides of the track, can be traced for nearly 1000 yards running along the side of a small stream until the latter meets the River Nene. Near the river, to the north of the track, is one Roman settlement, perhaps a single farm; to the south is a larger one, probably a small village. At the river a line of large posts was found in 1950 extending across the floodplain for about twenty-five yards beyond the end of the trackway. These, it has been suggested, may be the remains of a wooden bridge. On the east of the river the continuation of the trackway, if it ever existed, is not visible, but there is another Roman settlement there to which the trackway may have been leading.

An example of a different kind of local trackway may be seen in south-east Cambridgeshire, near the village of Swaffham Prior. There, on the fen edge, was a large Roman villa, discovered in the late nineteenth century. A few years ago the farmer noticed two parallel marks some fifteen yards apart in his barley crop, extending from the courtyard of the villa across the rising ground to the south-east for about a mile. This was interpreted as the main drive to the villa, but its continuation was unknown. Some time later, this drive or trackway was seen from the air and traced for a further two miles across the chalk downland until it met the line of the Icknield Way just south-west of Newmarket. This shows that the Way was still being used in Roman times; and from this kind of cumulative evidence we are gradually beginning to see the complex pattern of local trackways which covered Roman Britain.

Until relatively recently much more complex systems of Roman tracks were still visible on the ground in many places on the chalk downlands of southern England. Now, as a result of the demands of

twentieth-century agriculture, these downlands have been ploughed
up and most of the trackways destroyed. This writer was fortunate
enough to examine some of them before they were finally ploughed
away. One place was on the northern side of a broad valley near
Maiden Newton in Dorset (Fig. 37), where a narrow terraced track
appeared out of the modern arable land and ran along the edge of
the valley between small Roman fields. It passed through a group of
banks and ditches marking the site of a Roman farmstead and then a
few yards beyond entered another farmstead. There it forked. One
branch turned north-east across the downlands, passed through yet
another farmstead and ran on as a slight holloway until it disappeared into the modern ploughland again, just short of the
Dorchester-Ilchester Roman road which it undoubtedly joined. The
other branch ran south-east down the hillside as a broad terrace
with Roman fields on either side. Just before it reached the existing
cultivated land, a side track left it at a T-junction, climbed up the
steep hillside and joined the other branch of the track on the summit
of the downs. This remarkable survival showed clearly how complex
the Roman countryside really was and how many miles of trackways
must have existed all over Britain. Today such examples are rare
and even the remains of the Roman farms and villages survive in
only a few places.

Nevertheless some of these Roman rural settlements do show, even
if less spectacularly than the previous example, how many trackways
there were. Again in Dorset, on the end of a high chalk spur north of
Milton Abbas, is one of the best-preserved Roman villages in Britain
(Fig. 38). It is remarkable for a number of reasons, not the least
because it shows that the built-up area of the village was completely
delimited by a low bank, surrounded by a large open area which one
might call a 'green', though in fact it was outside the village, not in
its centre. The 'green' itself is also bounded by a bank beyond which
are the remains of the small rectangular fields of the village. More
important, from our point of view, four separate tracks run through
these fields, each leading into the village green. From the west
comes a broad embanked holloway, from the north-west a narrower
embanked holloway, from the north a similar one while from the
south-east, climbing up the hillside, is a wide curving terrace
(Plate IV). We have no idea where all these tracks led to, for later
farmers have removed all traces. The south-eastern terrace way may
have climbed up the next spur 700 yards away where there is

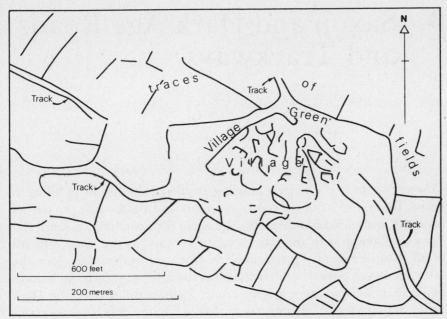

Fig. 38 Roman village, fields and tracks, Milton Abbas, Dorset

another Roman village with one of its three trackways pointing towards this one. But this is just supposition and we cannot be sure. We can only marvel that enough remains for us at least to appreciate what the Roman landscape was actually like.

As with many of the prehistoric trackways discussed in the first chapter, we must not ignore the possibility that many of our roads and lanes originated from these Roman tracks. There is no way of proving this, however, and the undoubted attractions of linking known Roman tracks to existing roads and so building up a completely specious system of routeways needs to be avoided at all costs.

We may thus summarize the story of Roman roads and tracks as being one of high complexity. They seem to have extended to all parts of the country linking settlements, towns and fields together in a remarkable way. The whole of the British landscape appears to have been criss-crossed by tracks and roads, which not only brought Roman civilization to the remotest corners of that land, but also allowed the exploitation of the countryside to an extent which perhaps has not been exceeded until the twentieth century.

# 3 Saxon and Dark Age Roads and Trackways

Whatever aspect of the past is being studied, whether it be villages, farms, fields, forests or, in our case, roads and trackways, the period from the end of Roman times in the early fifth century AD, until the Norman Conquest in the late eleventh century, is the most difficult of all to understand. Obviously it is less well understood than the later medieval period, and it may be thought, correctly as it happens, that there is more known about Roman times than the Dark Ages. But it is odd, though true, that we know much more about Bronze Age villages, fields and indeed trackways than we know of Saxon ones. For anyone who is interested in the history of the British landscape, the Saxon period remains largely a blank. As modern scholars have looked, with increasing skill and care, at the history of the Dark Ages, they have realized that though most of the old ideas about the landscape of that period can be discounted, they have consistently failed to reveal the true picture.

Even ten years ago, for example, it was generally believed that the typical nucleated village of medieval, and indeed modern England was established by early Saxon settlers who then surrounded it by open or common fields, made up of unhedged strips, through which passed roads or lanes to the next village. And beyond the limits of the Saxon invaders, in Scotland, Wales and south-west England, hard-pressed groups of Celtic survivors struggled on in the older way of life, living in isolated farmsteads and using the Roman system of tracks.

Now we can no longer be sure that this was so. Certainly English villages, as we now see them, are not early Saxon; they seem to have appeared many centuries later. Likewise the open field systems were not brought into Britain fully developed by Saxon settlers. They apparently grew up many centuries afterwards in response to complex social, economic and agricultural changes. And in the uplands

of the north and the west of Britain, far from there being groups of
Celtic-speaking survivors living in an old-fashioned and backward
society, there were in fact highly sophisticated peoples, with long-
range contacts, not only with their Saxon neighbours but with most
of western Europe, living in all types of settlements and cultivating
kinds of fields which we certainly cannot recognize at the moment.

Herein lies the problem for those of us interested in the history of
roads and tracks. In earlier periods, even in the Bronze Age, we know
something of the size and location of settlements and thus can infer
much of the communication system that existed. In later times we
know a great deal about the location, size and shape of the settlements and thus, together with the actual roads, can understand the
pattern of routeways. But in the Dark Ages or early Saxon period,
we are not even sure where the settlements were and we certainly
have no known roads which we can date to these times. Therefore
even a tentative understanding of the roads and tracks of these dark
centuries must be based on the most insubstantial evidence. This
chapter will attempt to interpret this evidence, but it must be clearly
understood at the outset how little we actually know and how much
we must guess.

Towards the end of the fourth century AD Roman Britain came
under increasing attack from outside raiders. These comprised not
only Saxons from north-west Europe, but people from Ireland and
areas of Scotland beyond the Roman frontier. In previous centuries
such raids could have been easily contained, but by this time the
fabric of the Empire was crumbling as a result of internal political
pressures and economic problems. Thus it became more and more
difficult for the Empire to keep a firm hold on an outlying province
which was under attack. Some attempts were made to protect Britain, including the building of a complex series of coastal forts, but
not all the raids could be stemmed and one particular large-scale
attack on all parts of the country occurred in 367 AD. This invasion
was repulsed, though not before the raiders had caused widespread
destruction over a great part of the country. One aspect of this event
which is directly reflected in the history of the roads of this period
was found in an excavation of a large defensive bank and ditch
known as Bokerley Dyke which runs for four miles across the downlands on the Hampshire-Dorset border. At one point this dyke cuts
across the Roman road from Salisbury to Dorchester. The excavation showed that when the dyke was built in the late fourth century

AD it was erected across the road and so blocked it. It has been plausibly suggested that this event relates to the attack of 367 and was an attempt to stop Saxon raiders, who had reached Wiltshire and Hampshire, from driving south into Dorset. The blocking was soon removed and the road repaired, but this reveals clearly how disruptive of communications were such invasions, a feature which was to recur on a vast scale very soon afterwards.

Though the major invasions of 367 were successfully repulsed, the attacks from outside continued on an increasing scale and the Roman army, on which Britain depended for its defence, was whittled down as successive political crises and rebellions at the heart of the Empire drew troops from the outlying provinces. In 407 the last regular Roman troops were withdrawn and the population of Britain was left to fend for itself, a situation which was formalized in 410. Thus without a central administration, with the major economic links with the rest of Europe broken, with no defences and under constant external attack, the internal economy, trade, industry and communications collapsed. Society itself disintegrated into local political units and petty kingdoms who eventually spent as much time fighting each other as they did the raiders from without. Not that the collapse of Roman Britain was sudden or accepted without a struggle. Various attempts were made to rebuild a central government and to a certain extent the raiders were kept at bay, if only by using some of them as mercenary troops. But a little before 450 not only did the mercenaries revolt but a new phase of development began, in eastern England at least. There the raiders from northwest Europe were replaced by settlers looking for land. This produced even more pressure on the already unstable Roman society, which finally disintegrated, and the great system of roads it had supported was largely abandoned.

The details of this abandonment are not entirely clear. We have a few pieces of direct evidence, but most we can only guess at. One indication of the collapse of the road system can again be seen at Bokerley Dyke on the Hampshire-Dorset border, for the excavation which showed that the Roman road there was blocked by the dyke, perhaps in 367, and was then reopened, also showed that at a later date, presumably when new danger threatened, the dyke was rebuilt across the road, closing it again, this time for ever. This is one of only a handful of examples showing the deliberate end of a Roman road. In most places there is no such evidence, nor perhaps should we expect it. Most main Roman roads probably gradually fell out of use, except perhaps for short lengths used by local traffic, as the need for and the basis of long-distance communication declined. With this decline must have gone the cessation of repair work on the roads, which in turn restricted movement along them even more. Probably the wooden bridges were the first to go, their timber uprights rotted by water and finally swept away in winter storms. Fords would be removed as the rivers reverted to their natural courses, while culverts were first blocked and then torn out by floods. In the uplands soil slips and washouts would have put numerous barriers along many roads and in wooded areas fallen trees probably soon prevented any movement. Once these major breaks occurred, and the traffic stopped, then the road surfaces would have been broken by frost and rain, and vegetation would invade the aggers.

Thus with communications gone and Britons fighting Saxons, as well as divided among themselves, most movement took place along purely local tracks. In the past the post-Roman period has been pictured as one of hordes of incoming Saxon invaders pouring across the countryside, sweeping all before them and thus of necessity using either the lines of the old Roman roads, or being reduced to following the old so-called prehistoric trackways to gain access into Britain. But the reality was probably very different. Certainly after AD 450 when the itinerant raiders were replaced by settlers who were mainly concerned with acquiring land for agriculture, there is no indication of massive, well-organized movement along roads or tracks of any kind. More likely there was a gradual infiltration of new peoples, in small groups, fighting for new land here, living in uneasy peace side by side with Britons there and everywhere intermarrying and settling down to a routine agricultural life. If routes were used at all it is probable that rivers rather than trackways were the main lines of movement and certainly the distribution of early Saxon burial sites in eastern and southern England suggests that the Thames, Ouse and Trent were more important than the old trackways at this time.

One specific area where there seems, at first sight, to be evidence of massive movement along old trackways is in southern Cambridgeshire, where the broad chalkland strip between the forested claylands to the south and the fens to the north is spanned by a series of great ditches, the largest being the famous Devil's Dyke. These, though undated, are later than the Roman period and earlier than the seventh century AD. From two of them comes evidence of fighting involving Saxon peoples and they have often been interpreted as blocking ditches to stop movement along the Icknield Way thus proving that the latter was in use at this time as a major through route. However they are far more likely to represent frontier boundaries of various territories held by either Saxons or Britons along which battles occurred. The Saxon settlers in the area whose cemeteries and burial places have been discovered are far more likely to have arrived by boat along the fenland rivers which gave easy access to the region. The so-called Grimms Ditches of the Chiltern Hills in Buckinghamshire and Oxfordshire, some of which appear also to block the Icknield Way there, may have the same origin as frontiers.

By the end of the sixth century AD much of lowland England had been settled by Saxons, and in the next century these people advanced into the far south-west as well as across the uplands of northern England. As farmers seeking land their first objective was to find a place to live and territory to cultivate. Until recently we have confidently assumed that the way in which this was done was to establish large nucleated villages – in fact those that exist today – around which they laid out their ubiquitous common or strip fields. These villages, by their very shape which we can still see, imply a pattern of tracks, either already then in being or created by the establishment of the villages themselves. Thus when we see a village made up of houses strung out on either side of a single main street it is a plausible assumption to say that there was an earlier road or track along which the first Saxons built their houses. Similarly when we find a village centred on a neat triangular green it is apparently obvious that the roads or tracks radiating from that green were established by the early Saxon farmers moving out into their surrounding fields, or as routes to the next settlement. Now while these assumptions may be true, it is very doubtful that the early Saxons actually did this. For, as a result of recent archaeological research, it seems that the typical English village, as we know it, was a product of later centuries, and had little to do with the early Saxon settlers at all.

The evidence for this is complex and as this book is not directly concerned with the history of Saxon villages we cannot go into all the detail. Very briefly, the pattern of early Saxon settlement is, perhaps surprisingly, similar to the Roman one, and in many

respects is related to it. There were no major nucleated villages two
or three miles apart, but countless small farmsteads and hamlets
dotted about all over the countryside. One specific example of this
must suffice. In the parish of Great Doddington, in Northamptonshire, where in later medieval times there was, and indeed still is, a
single large village centred on the parish church, we now know that
in the early Saxon period there were at least nine, and probably
more, small farms or hamlets scattered all over the parish. Elsewhere
such places have been excavated. These show that the typical
Saxon settlement was far removed from the medieval village both in
form and probably in location. The farmsteads consisted of little
more than two or three huts, while the hamlets seem to have been
made up of groups of timber houses, sometimes well built, but with
no clearly definable layout, and certainly no indication of any relationship to trackways. Just as important, when archaeological excavations are carried out in existing villages, or more easily on villages
which have been abandoned in the late or post-medieval period,
either no occupation before the tenth or eleventh centures has been
found, or, where Saxon material is present, it is entirely unrelated to
the present village or its roads and tracks. Quite apart from the
implications of this new evidence for the history of settlement in England, it makes our task of understanding early Saxon roads almost
impossible for we thus have no evidence for them at all. We can only
suggest that the countless Roman rural trackways, which we looked
at in the last chapter, continued to be used by the Saxon farmers.
Indeed this is quite likely, for if we can stray into yet another aspect
of these dark centuries and look at Saxon fields we may obtain some
clues. As was mentioned above, the typical medieval strip-field system did not come with the Saxons. It was developed gradually over
many centuries. The first Saxon settlers must have cultivated the
existing fields of the Romano-Britons. Later on, as population rose
and different agricultural practices evolved, these Roman fields may
have been subdivided into strips and cultivated in common. We
have some evidence for this, in that recent examination of ditches,
lying below the later boundaries between the furlongs or blocks of
strips in medieval fields, has shown that many are of Roman date
and thus presumably bounded Roman fields. As we already know
that these fields were, in Roman times, bisected and bounded by
contemporary trackways linking them to the Roman farmsteads,
hamlets, villas and villages, then we may perhaps with some justifi-

cation say that the Saxon famers also used these tracks for the same purpose.

Here of course we have the strong possibility of even longer continuity. If we are correct in saying that the Roman fields became Saxon fields, which when subdivided into strips evolved into true medieval common fields, probably many of the trackways through the medieval fields, most of which existed until quite recently, and some of which still remain in use today, can be considered to be at least Roman in origin. We shall look at these in more detail in the next chapter. Thus, though the details are unknown, we must perhaps think once more of the probability that many of our existing roads are of very great antiquity, even if we cannot date them.

When we move into those parts of Britain which the Saxons did not reach, or on which they had little influence, it is even more difficult to find Dark Age roads and tracks. Once again the problem of dating any road that is not deliberately constructed appears. The upland areas of south-west England, Wales and Scotland are crisscrossed by tracks and trails, but there is no way of dating them because they were obviously used for many centuries. A detailed study of the old trackways in the Cheviot Hills of south-east Scotland, for example, has produced no evidence of period, only of long continuous use. They consist typically of sets of alternate hollowed tracks, evidently worn by the passage of men and animals, which run side by side, criss-cross among themselves and spread out or contract into wider or narrower belts as the lie of the land dictates. One of the most interesting is that called The Street which crosses the Cheviots from the River Coquet to the Kale Water. We know that much of it was still in use in the nineteenth century, and indeed people still alive remember loads of oatmeal being carted along it to supply isolated shepherds on the English side of the border. On the other hand careful examination has revealed that many of the ruts and hollows can be shown to overlie a simple trackway less then twenty feet across. This, together with a possible reference to it in a twelfth-century charter, suggests that this track may be of Dark Age origin. On the other hand, it might equally well be considerably older.

The only possible way of ever understanding the tracks and roads of this period is to identify settlements to which they were related. As we have seen already in England, this is an insuperable task because we do not yet know in enough detail where the Saxon settlements were. In the north and west of Britain this task is somewhat easier for the scattered pattern of farmsteads and hamlets is, as far as we can see, very old indeed and certainly in part of Dark Age date. Even so, in a period where little was written down it is still very difficult to be sure of the situation. A good example of what may be done can be seen on the island of Anglesey, where an important study of medieval settlements in the south-west of the island has been carried out in order to ascertain the tenurial relationships between them. As the only documents detailed enough to give us the names and thus the locations of all the inhabited places there are of the thirteenth and fourteenth centuries we only achieve in the first instance the distribution of settlement at that time. However, the complex tenurial relationships between the lord, the Church and the tenant farmers in the farmsteads and hamlets can be shown to be directly related to a much older system of land tenure which may be dated to before the seventh century AD. Thus the scattered pattern of hamlets and farmsteads, which is recorded in the thirteenth century and which can still be seen, probably existed in much the same form in the Dark Ages.

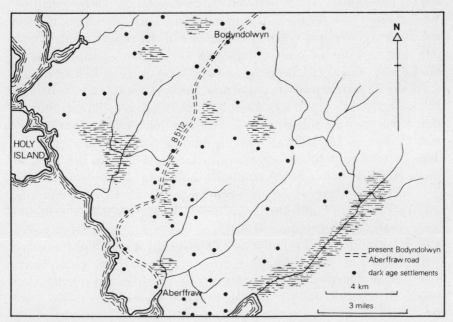

Fig. 39 Dark Age settlements in south-west Anglesey

If we now turn to the land in question we can identify in the present landscape thirty-four places known as vills (or townships) and hamlets which are likely to be of Dark Age date (Fig. 39). The former are dispersed groups of farmsteads and sometimes rather more compact village-type settlements. As they still exist, so do the roads and tracks which link them. These vary from main A class roads across Anglesey, down through minor B roads to country lanes and unmade farm tracks. None, of course, probably look as they did in the Dark Ages, neither would we expect them to. They have been altered in detail, reconstructed, straightened and built up, especially in recent times. But nonetheless they are the routes used by Dark Age people, or even earlier ones, as they went about their business.

So today if we go to this part of Anglesey we can still drive along these Dark Age routeways. We know that in the fourteenth century, and presumably for centuries before, one of the duties of men holding land in the vill of Bodyndolwyn, a group of farms west of the village of Llanerchymedd, was to repair the lord's Hall and Chamber at Aberffraw, a village some ten miles away on the coast. The obvious route between these two places, in order to avoid the low-lying marshy valleys, is that which at least in part today is the winding B5112 and A4080 road between Llanerchymedd and Aberffraw. This, though now far from its original form, must have been the way the Dark Age tenants reached the centre of the manor. This is only one instance out of many thousands of similar examples, but it does show, once again, both the age and long usage of British roads.

As the centuries passed, important changes took place in Britain. In political terms there was a gradual move towards larger units, so that tribes became sub-kingdoms, sub-kingdoms became major ones and finally, in England at least, a unified political state emerged. This increasing political organization inevitably led to the need for more complex administration, justice and general government control, including warfare, on an even larger scale. In economic and social terms these political changes were accompanied by developing trade, both within Britain and with the rest of Europe, and considerably more mobility of population. As a result, inevitably, trackways were developed and, perhaps much more important, older routes again used. Once more the problems of defining these tracks and roads are considerable, probably because in most areas the rural trackways already in use for centuries continued to be traversed, the only difference being that part of the traffic moved beyond the confines of the villages or farmsteads they had previously served, and thus became part of a larger national system.

The documentary evidence for the general growth of these roads is very slight. In England at least the innumerable Saxon land charters which survive from the eighth century onwards often refer to 'wegs' or ways along the boundaries of the territories they were defining. But few specify what sort of way. There are some exceptions to this. One fairly common road name in Saxon charters is that of *Here-paeth*, a military road, or rather a track used primarily for military purposes. It is still not entirely clear how such a name arose. Some Here-paeths appear to lead to the sites of well-known battles, and as such may merely reflect the tradition that soldiers connected with that battle once marched along it. On the other hand the name may mean tracks which were regularly used by forces of warring kingdoms or were followed by government administrators travelling with armed escorts. Either way it is probable that such tracks were used by other people, and for the same reason, to travel distances beyond the normal limits of local economic and social demand.

If we accept this latter interpretation then it is possible to identify some of these long-distance tracks, although the dangers of linking up isolated occurrences of the name and so producing spurious major routeways has to be avoided. In Wiltshire, for example, there is a rutted track some seven miles long across the Marlborough Downs between Avebury and Marlborough, part of which in Saxon times was called a *Here-paeth*. It is very easy to take a map and, by joining up various roads and tracks which seem to meet it, reconstruct the Saxon roads of the area and especially connect them with the great ridgeways leading north-east to East Anglia and south across Salisbury Plain. While this might well be true, we have no evidence for it at all, and the Here-paeth here might just as easily be a minor branch of the London-Bath road, the present A4, which runs along the Kennet Valley a little to the south. This latter idea is not necessarily as unsubstantiated as it seems, for the Here-paeth certainly had just that purpose in medieval times and even up to the eighteenth century.

Another common description given to a road in Saxon land charters is *straet*. It is again not certain what this word meant, but it is usually assumed to be a deliberately constructed road as opposed to a track where the words way, weg or here-paeth were used. If this is so then most *straets* should be Roman roads and this is the case in some places. However, there is one problem with this word straet. As a made Roman road was an obvious feature in the landscape and its purpose clearly understood, it would be given the name whether it was used as a road at the time or not. Therefore the occurrence of the term may not be telling us about the road system of Saxon times at all, but only about the existence of a feature in the landscape. The same might apply to other terms. A here-paeth may have been called that because of a tradition or legend, for example, whether true or not, that a visible track was once used as such. It does not necessarily mean that it was used as a trackway in Saxon times. The Saxons often gave fanciful names to features which appeared to be of great antiquity and which they did not understand. Wansdyke in Wiltshire, that is Woden's Ditch, the numerous Grimm's Ditches and even Devil's Dyke are all examples of illogical names given to features in the landscape which were of unknown date and purpose. Even in later periods the same situation existed. The numerous Danes' Holes, Dykes, Ways and Hills, and even Cromwell's Batteries, Seats, Trees, etc. all show how people give spurious names of high antiquity to features they cannot understand. A disused or little used trackway running for miles across the countryside might easily be given the name military way (here-paeth) for the same reasons.

In other parts of Britain, various efforts have been made to identify Dark Age tracks with little success, usually because of the total lack of evidence to date them. In Glamorgan, for example, a scholarly attempt to do this shows the problem only too well. There the existence of Dark Age roads and tracks is obvious, as it is elsewhere, but it is impossible to pinpoint them. Clearly only the ancient-looking trackways over the mountains have any chance of being dated, but even there, where every ridge top is crossed by tracks and holloways, it is extremely difficult to say that one is of Dark Age date, another prehistoric and a third medieval. All are of many periods, the result of long-distance and local traffic over thousands of years. In a few places there appear to be dykes across ridges which block or control trackways. There is a splendid example to the north of Swansea on the hill of Tor Clawdd where a long curving bank and ditch block a very ancient-looking trackway. These dykes cannot be dated at all, but they are said to be of ninth-century origin on somewhat dubious grounds. Yet even if they are of this date, they show only that the tracks were finally abandoned then; they do not tell us whether the

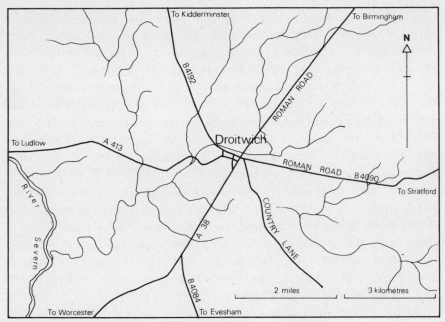

Fig. 40 Dark Age salt ways, Droitwich, Worcestershire

route is prehistoric, Roman or Dark Age in origin. Another possible indication of Dark Age roads in Wales is the distribution of inscribed stones of seventh- to ninth-century date along upland tracks. Again this might show that these were in use at that time, but as the stones usually have religious significance, they may be unconnected with the tracks. In any case they tell us nothing of the origins of these mountain ways.

A far more useful indication of long-distance routes in Saxon or Dark Age times is the term saltway. Salt was then, and always has been, a basic necessity of life and thus trade in the material was important. In Saxon times, as well as the salterns along the coasts, the two major inland industrial centres were Droitwich in Worcestershire and Northwich in Cheshire. From these two places a large number of roads radiate, all recorded as saltways in medieval or earlier times. If we look at one of these salt-producing centres we can to some extent see the network of roads which carried the product over long distances. We know, for example, that Droitwich was producing salt at an early date in the Saxon period, for around the middle of the eighth century King Ethelbald of Mercia gave to the

Church of Worcester a plot of ground there for the construction of three salt-houses and six furnaces. In addition, and much more important, it is possible to identify many of the actual saltways on the ground today (Fig. 40). The result might disconcert those who still think that Saxon trackways are the present green lanes of England, but by now we should not be surprised to find that all are still well used today. Of the six identifiable Saxon saltways leading out from Droitwich, those to the south-west and north-east are the present A38 road between Worcester and Birmingham, here also a Roman road, one is the present road north-west to Kidderminster, one the main road west to Ludlow and another, a second Roman road, runs east to Stratford. Only the last of these roads is not a major route at the present time, but even so it comprises a group of three busy country lanes leading from the town to adjacent villages. The main saltway to the south-east actually left the Droitwich to Worcester road a little to the south-west of the town and its line is still the main road to Evesham.

By the end of the eighth century Britain was organized into well-defined kingdoms, albeit often at war with each other, which for economic, administrative or military reasons were developing a new long-distance system of communications. This owed only a little to the earlier Roman pattern. The last centuries before the Norman Conquest saw major changes in the political and economic basis of British society which, as always, was reflected in the road system of the country. In England at least the emergence of a unified state, following the Danish invasions of the ninth century, inevitably speeded up the growth of long-distance routes. Even more important this period saw the development of towns again, for the first time since the end of Roman rule. Though some of the older Roman towns continued to be occupied, they did not function as towns in an economic sense and thus cannot be called such. Perhaps the word *development* is wrong, for it implies what most people perhaps think of as the origin of towns, that is, slow growth from an existing village on a good site. In fact the first English towns were not the result of gradual development: they were newly planted at specific places, usually in the first instance for military reasons, and later for economic and administrative ones. Not all these plantations were successful, for ultimately the economic pressures of market forces decided which places were to develop and which to decline, but the origins of these towns were the result of a deliberate human decision, not a gift given by a gracious Nature to chosen places. The earliest towns were probably the fortresses, erected first by King Alfred to protect his Kingdom of Wessex from the Danes, and later by the Danes themselves as military and political centres. Thus the sites of these fortresses, or burghs as they were called, were based on strategic and tactical military considerations. Their success or otherwise as towns came later when their function changed and they became marketing centres. Those that were not well situated for the latter purpose tended to decline, while those well sited developed.

Usually, but not always of course, a good military site is probably a good commercial one, and the vital route centres which need to be controlled and guarded by a fort would also aid the growth of a town. Thus many of the fortresses with which King Alfred encircled and divided his kingdom grew to be successful towns, including such places as Shaftesbury and Wareham in Dorset, Wilton· and Cricklade in Wiltshire, and Wallingford in Oxfordshire. Others, such as Lydford in Devon, though successful both as forts and, at first, as towns, later declined to villages. Some, for example, Burpham near Arundel, never advanced beyond small settlements, while others were abandoned at the end of their military life and were never resettled. One of the latter, near Little Bredy in Dorset, is now just an earthen rampart encircling a deserted hill top. The forts built by the Danes have, for various reasons, survived as towns rather better than the English ones. Derby, Nottingham, Leicester, Bedford and Stamford are among those which became important medieval urban areas. All these successful forts/towns acquired not only an administrative importance, but also became the main economic centres of the country. Links were established between them, trade encouraged and, as a result, roads to and from them developed. It is worthwhile looking at two or three of these new towns to see how they changed or were changed by the road systems; one town which shows well the effect on the existing road pattern of a military fort of this period is Stamford in Lincolnshire (Fig. 41).

As a result of very detailed topographical and archaeological work we can be fairly sure of the sequence of roads at Stamford. In the Roman period, apart from a scatter of farmsteads, there was no major occupation of the area. The main Roman road, the Ermine Street, ran in long straight alignments from Durobrivae, the Roman town to the south on the River Nene, to Great Casterton, another Roman town some three miles to the north-west of the present Stam-

ford. The Ermine Street crossed the River Welland upstream from
where Stamford now stands, in a broad open valley. At the end of
the Roman period, the Ermine Street was probably made unusable
by the collapse of the bridge. The earliest Saxon settlement in the
area seems to have been a little downstream from the Roman bridge
and the way across the river here was at a point where the river was
flowing in a series of shallow channels which could be forded easily.
Thus the Saxon settlement on the north side of this crossing took the
name stony ford or Stamford. In about AD 877 the Danish army
gained control of this part of Lincolnshire and found it necessary to
build a fort or burgh to control this ford. For tactical reasons the
best place for the fort was just to the east of the Saxon settlement, on
a generally flat terrace overlooking both river crossing and the Saxon
village and with its main gate leading on to the main through-road
climbing the hillside from the ford. Thus the establishment of this
fort caused no immediate change in the route pattern established by
the Saxons.

However in 918 King Edward the Elder, as part of his reconquest
of the area from the Danes, took Stamford and ordered 'the burgh on

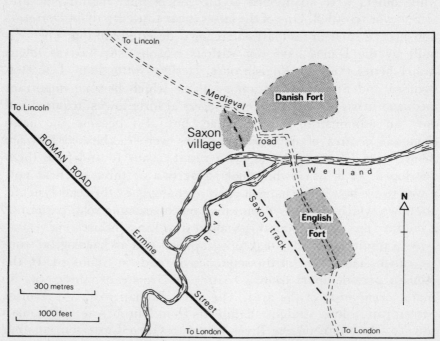

Fig. 41 Roman, Saxon and medieval roads, Stamford, Lincolnshire

the south side of the river to be built'. This new English fort was erected alongside the road to the ford and slightly askew to it. Both Danish and English forts grew into a town and the whole became one of the most important places in eastern England by the eleventh century. The town had a mint, for instance and the number of people officially allowed to produce coinage was only exceeded in towns such as London, York, Winchester and Lincoln. The result of this prosperity and trade was that the road system changed, the old route to the ford was abandoned and a new one developed which ran down the main street of the English burgh, across the river at a point narrow enough for a new bridge to carry it and up on to the terrace of the Danish burgh. The road then passed round the Danish burgh and turned back on to its original alignment to the north of the town. Thus in a space of some 600 years the crossing of the River Welland moved gradually downstream from the Roman bridge via the Saxon ford to the English bridge.

It is not without interest in the history of roads to look briefly at later changes on this road; which ultimately became the main route from London to the north, now the A1 trunk road. The diversion from the direct Saxon route to the one through the two forts produced three sharp bends on the north side of the river. Though adequate for medieval and later times, by the 1950s this was totally inadequate. The increase in motor transport after the Second World War along the narrow streets of Stamford threatened to choke the town to death. As a result the A1 bypass was built to the west, this time changing the river crossing yet again on to a new alignment.

A slightly different picture of change and alteration to a road system with the development of a late Saxon town can be seen at Winchester (Fig. 42). Here, unlike Stamford, was a Roman city with major roads leading from it in all directions. At the end of the Roman period the town, though not abandoned, lost its urban function and became little more than a local ecclesiastical and market centre. But in 880–6 the town was replanned with a new street system as part of King Alfred's aim to make it the fortified capital of his Kingdom of Wessex. It soon developed into a major political, administrative and economic centre and as a result, produced a new system of roads leading to all parts of the kingdom and beyond. It is interesting to look at this road system and to see to what extent it relied on the older arrangement of Roman roads. The main route to the north-east and London still used the old Roman

line. The earlier road, running straight across open downland with
no collapsed bridges and blocked fords to make it impassable, and
leading in the desired direction at least as far as Basingstoke, clearly
could be reused with advantage. So too could the main road to the
south for a short distance, which was the Roman road to
Clausentum, a town which lay on the east side of the Itchen estuary
near Southampton. But four miles south of Winchester, at
Otterbourne, the Saxon road left the Roman one. This was because,
by this time, Clausentum was no longer in existence and had been
replaced by a port on the west side of the Itchen that was to become,
after a complex history, the town of Southampton. There was no
point in continuing south to cross the Itchen at a ferry near South
Stoneham, as the Roman road did, so the Saxon road turned at
Otterbourne and followed the line of another Roman road
south-west for three miles. Then, because that road was leading to
nowhere that was important, the road to Southampton was turned
south again and took a winding course into the port.

To the south-east of Winchester, a Roman road ran to Chichester.
By late Saxon times, however, there was not only no important traffic
on this route, but the road itself was crossing difficult country with a
whole series of steep climbs and descents. Thus, apart from the
immediate environs of Winchester itself, the Roman road was largely
abandoned and an easier, more circuitous route, took what traffic
there was to the south-east. On the east side of Winchester there
were no Roman roads, yet the Saxon capital needed communications
in this direction. Two somewhat winding roads therefore came into
existence, probably by linking up old trackways.

Two other roads left the Roman town of Winchester. One was to
the north-west, leading to the Roman town of Mildenhall in Wiltshire, the other a major route to Salisbury and the lead mines of the
Mendips in the west. The Mildenhall road was again used by the
Saxons for three or four miles, but as soon as its direction was no
longer suitable they turned off and continued north, thus establishing one of the major routes of medieval England to Oxford, Northampton and Stamford (now the A34 and A43 trunk roads). The
Roman road to the west was, oddly, amost completely abandoned.
Oddly not only because the road was easy to travel along, but also
because, just beyond Salisbury, there was another of King Alfred's
forts or burghs, Wilton. One can only conclude that the Roman road
was given up in the centuries between the collapse of Roman rule

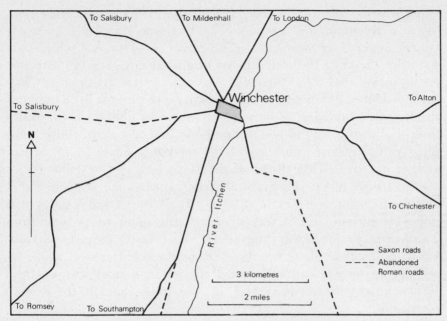

Fig. 42 Saxon and Roman roads, Winchester, Hampshire

and the founding and refounding of Wilton and Winchester so that when the time came for an important route to the west to develop, the Roman road line was forgotten and the new route followed existing local tracks crossing the River Test at Stockbridge, well to the north of the old road. This situation at Winchester shows, in some detail, why we still use some Roman roads today but not others. The ones which are still major routes are probably those which never went out of use completely, even though they were only local tracks in the Dark Ages. Those which disappeared either had no local function in early Saxon times, or were so impassable as a result of bridge collapses and washouts that no traffic could move along them.

Both the examples of late Saxon forts/towns discussed so far have been related, in part at least, to earlier Roman road systems. But some of these places were set down in areas where the system either never existed, or had no relationship to the new fort and its needs. One such is Tamworth in Staffordshire (Fig. 43). Tamworth had long been a place of some importance as the site of a palace of the kings of Mercia, but in 913 a fortress was erected there in order to protect the eastern frontier of that kingdom against the Danes. Its siting was to some extent the result of the earlier royal connection, but also because of local tactical considerations. As a consequence it entirely ignored the Roman Watling Street (now the A5) which passed it by 1½ miles to the south. Its origins as a royal administrative centre meant that the subsequent fort and its later development as a town produced a radiating pattern of roads which took little notice of the Roman road. Most of these roads still exist and are main routes from the town today, although one is no longer a main route but a pleasant green lane which leaves the modern road to Lichfield just after it has crossed the River Tame. This lane can be followed for just over three miles, as it gradually converges on the Watling Street and finally meets it near the village of Wall. As we see it today it is not very ancient, but it was probably the main route west from Tamworth in later Saxon times along which traffic moved via Tamworth rather than along the direct Roman road. Here yet again we see the mixture of continuity and change in a road system, from Roman road to Saxon track and, in later times, back to the Roman road again.

Before leaving the roads of these Dark Ages, we must look at some

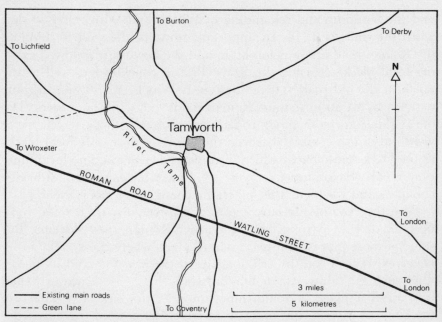

Fig. 43 Road system, Tamworth, Staffordshire

important evidence relating not just to the major routes, which have been our concern up to now, but to the total pattern of roads, lanes and tracks which by now covered the whole country. To do this we must return, briefly, to the story of the evolving settlement pattern. We saw that, in early Saxon times in England, and in Dark Age Wales and the north, villages as we know them did not exist. But in the eighth, ninth and tenth centuries, though the process was to go on later, the medieval village gradually appeared. At the moment we do not know how or why the change from a pattern of small farms or hamlets scattered over the countryside became the familiar arrangement of nucleated villages, arranged around greens, or along streets. The process may have been, in part at least, a deliberately planned one, for many villages have forms which can only be explained by assuming a deliberate and instantaneous decision either by a lord or by a group of people. The most likely explanation for the appearance of the nucleated village is that it was connected with the development of the medieval common fields, which also seem to have appeared in these centuries. It is possible that as the complex system of plough strips with their rigid regulations, crop rotation, animal folding, and the use of common pasture evolved, the settlements which went with these fields also emerged. It may be no accident that, in the areas of Britain where the medieval common fields either never developed or only partly evolved, the nucleated village is rare or non-existent.

The whole problem of the evolution of the village in Britain at this time is a complex one, and not our direct concern here. The most important aspect from our point of view is that as these villages grew up in late Saxon times, for whatever reason, they were directly related to the existing road system. As we have already seen, many parts of this system may have been centuries old by that time, formed by prehistoric animals, Bronze Age farmers or Roman estate managers. But now, for the first time, we can get a virtually complete picture. Let us look at some examples of this in order to see not only the complexity but also how it can reveal the basic road pattern. Even at the simplest level it seems difficult to understand but, in spite of this, the underlying route system is visible. In West Yorkshire, south-west of Wakefield, is the village of Flockton, lying on the north side of a small east-flowing stream (Fig. 44). At first sight it appears to be a village strung out along a single street, but if analysed carefully, it can be seen to be two separate villages, a long

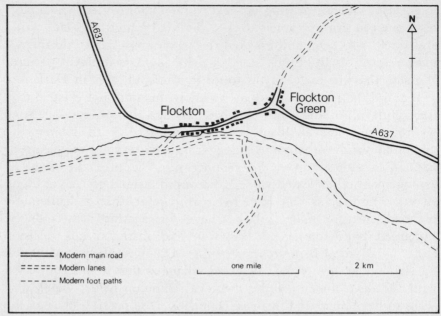

Fig. 44 Late Saxon road system, Flockton, Yorkshire

street village on the west and a small 'green' village to the east. It is
possible that the earliest village was along the street, and that the
green village came later. However, in a sense, this does not matter,
for what we have is clearly a situation in which there were, long
before the village developed, tracks on each side of and parallel to
the stream. Thus when the village was founded or developed it grew
up along the northern of these tracks. At both ends of the village,
tracks left the main one and ran up over the hillside into the next
valley. At the fork at the eastern end of the village, Flockton
Green, the other village, developed around the triangular area
whose form was defined by the Y-junction of the tracks. Thus the
basic pre-village layout of tracks in the area conditioned the form
of the villages when they finally appeared. Of course in later
centuries this pattern of tracks altered somewhat in response to
changes in land-use as well as in local and long-distance traffic. In
particular, the track on the south side of the stream declined in
importance and is now in part only a footpath. The same has
happened at the western end of the northern track. The latter was
overtaken in importance by the road forking off it to the north-west,

which is now the main road to Huddersfield and Brighouse. Nevertheless, not only is the original layout of tracks still visible and understandable but much of it is still used in one form or another.

Another, more complex, example can be seen at Canons Ashby in south-western Northamptonshire (Fig. 45). We appear to have no village here at all, only a great country house, a church and one farm, arranged around a curiously irregular pattern of roads. Yet there was a village, cleared away in the fourteenth century by a monastic house, in order to run great flocks of sheep on the land of that village. If we look carefully in the fields north of the great house, we can see the remains of the village, for there are the low banks and ditches of the original garden boundaries. From this we can see that the village was arranged along the two existing roads running north-east and north-west, with the priory to the south-east around the church. But if we go into the history of the village in more detail, we find that Canons Ashby House and its magnificent garden was not built until the sixteenth century, by which time the priory had disappeared. If we look at the land behind the house, to the south-west, we find the remains of a deeply hollowed track which appears

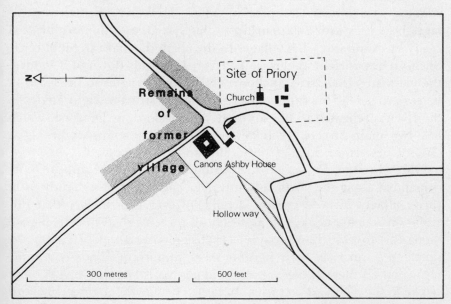

Fig. 45 Deserted village and existing roads, Canons Ashby, Northampton-shire

from under the boundary of the garden and runs down to meet the present lane running west to the next village. Then, suddenly, the pattern becomes clear. The village lay at a cross-roads where a north to south track crossed an east to west one. The priory, when it was founded here in 1147, occupied the south-east quadrant and thus priory and village lay side by side. Then in the fourteenth century the village was removed, and a century and a half later the priory disappeared and was replaced by Canons Ashby House. The gardens were then laid out about the house, the road running west from the cross-roads was blocked, and the curious loop to the south constructed to allow traffic to bypass the house and gardens. Here we see how complex the development of a small piece of countryside can be, but at the same time we can see that in spite of many changes and minor alterations of the road system the basic and original pre-village layout is still there and is still partly used.

So far we have looked at only single villages in order to see the pre-village road arrangement, but in many places the whole communications pattern of the area can be recovered by careful study. This can be done in south Cambridgeshire along the River Cam (Fig. 46). The present main road system is based on two roads, one on each side of, and parallel to, the river, with one major cross-road running east to west (the present A505). However, the existing villages bear very little relationship to this system and this can be seen easily by examining each village. In the north the main street of Little Shelford lies at right angles to the river, and leads down to it to meet the main street of Great Shelford, also at right angles to the river on its eastern side. This same pattern of a main street at right angles to the river is repeated to the south at Whittlesford, at Duxford, which has two main streets, at Ickleton and, further south in Essex, at Great Chesterford, Little Chesterford and Littlebury.

Only Hinxton, Pampisford, Sawston and Stapleford appear to be orientated along the north to south river-edge road. If we study these three villages in even greater detail, however, we can see that this situation was not always so and that all three were also once aligned along east to west tracks. Each has subsequently developed along the north to south road as it became more important. Thus it is quite clear that all these villages grew up along roads running east to west, crossing the Cam at a series of fords; hence the names Shelford (shallow ford), Whittlesford (Whittle's ford), Stapleford (Stone ford), and Chesterford (the ford by the Roman camp or town). Therefore it seems that the late Saxon road system was different from the present one only in the relative importance of its constituent parts. Most of the late Saxon east to west roads are still there, though, over the centuries, they have greatly changed both in form and function. The continuation of the main street of Little Shelford, for example, survives as a minor lane which has been pushed sideways by later development. The continuation of Whittleford's main street also

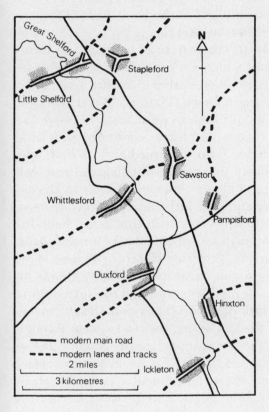

Fig. 46 Saxon villages and roads, south Cambridgeshire

exists, but now only as a public footpath to the next village and as a farm access track, though it was a through road until the beginning of the nineteenth century. One of the two roads west of Duxford is also there, a straight lane, given its present form in 1820. The other remained a farm lane until the 1940s when an airfield destroyed it. The same applies to the other villages where the original Saxon routes can all be seen. So eventually we can reconstruct the Saxon road system for a broad area of country, not as a result of wild guesses, or by drawing straight lines over a map, but by walking the land and deciphering the palimpsest which is there to be seen. All that has happened since the first villages were established in this area is exactly what has happened to roads and tracks throughout the ages. They have been adapted to meet changing traffic conditions, communication patterns and economic circumstances, but the basic framework has remained.

Once again we have so far tended to ignore the remoter parts of Britain in this study of roads at the end of the Dark Ages. The very use of the term Saxon implies this. In part this is because, in south-west England and Wales at least, the pattern of hamlets and farmsteads, linked by winding lanes which we can still traverse, can be shown to have been in existence even earlier than the late Saxon roads in lowland England discussed above (Plate V). Nevertheless, it is perhaps worth looking at one of these western areas to prove the point that the arrangement of roads and tracks continued with little change from late Roman times into the medieval period and beyond. To do this let us go down into south-west England and look at the countryside in the rolling hills north-west of Exeter in Devon. Here we have pre-Saxon England still in being. Villages are rare, and every part of the landscape is covered with tiny fields, bounded by massive hedge banks, with small farmsteads dotted among them. As a result of the pioneer work by Professor Hoskins, we now know that almost every one of the existing farmsteads actually stands on the site it occupied in the late eleventh century, and the surrounding fields too are of at least late Dark Age date. Thus as both settlements and fields are a stable part of the landscape, the road system through these fields, to and from the farmsteads, must equally be of eleventh-century date. We can see this well if we look at a typical area of Devon and take as our example the manor of Rashleigh in the hills on the western side of the River Taw between Barnstaple and Exeter (Fig. 47). The boundaries of the original eleventh-century manor of Rashleigh can still be traced on the ground and within them are six isolated farmsteads, and a small group of cottages in a remote corner. Detailed analysis of Domesday Book and later documents has shown that there were, in 1086, six individual farms, all of which can be identified with the present ones. The cottages are apparently where five smallholders were living at that time. Given that the fields around these farms today are virtually the same as they were in the eleventh century, which is extremely likely,

then the narrow lanes and tracks which wander along the hill tops
and slide down the steep valley sides, must be of that date too. Thus
today if we drive south across the River Taw at Kersham Bridge,
along the winding lane which climbs up and over a broad flat spur
and then down towards Heywood House, not only is every farm we
pass of at least eleventh-century date, but we are actually on a road
which was in use then.

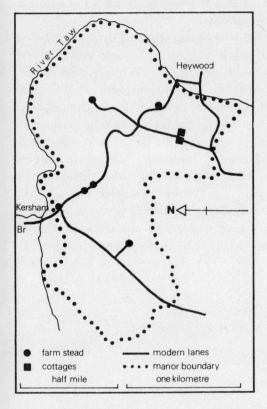

● farm stead  ——— modern lanes
■ cottages  • • • • manor boundary
half mile  one kilometre

Fig. 47 Late Saxon farms
and roads, Rashleigh,
Devon

   As Professor Hoskins has rightly said, if we could have a map of
rural Devon in the eleventh century it would look very like the modern Ordnance Survey map. 'Practically all the thousands of farm
names printed on the modern map would have been on the earlier
map, could it have been drawn; and nearly all the thousands of miles
of lanes and by-roads would have existed also.' The same is probably true of large areas of Cornwall, Wales and the Marches, and
much of northern England and Scotland. Yet if these farmsteads and
routes were there in the eleventh century, how much earlier are they?

Once again we do not know, but there is no reason to doubt that most of them would have been there in the Roman period, and some perhaps many centuries before. Indeed, though impossible to prove, certainly if we follow the Roman road from Exeter, north-west via Crediton towards Barnstaple, especially as it runs along the high land west of the River Taw, it seems to be superimposed on the surrounding pattern of lanes, most of which criss-cross the area as if the Roman road did not exist. If this is really so, then we see here a prehistoric road system, not an eleventh-century one.

It is this picture of the total road system, that we can see in being over most of Britain by the eleventh century, that makes this period so important in the history of roads and tracks. Whatever its origin, whether prehistoric, Roman or Dark Age, our present road system was virtually complete by this time and apart from the modern motorways and a few new roads in particular areas, our pattern of roads is the same as it was 900 years ago. In detail of course there have been many changes and minor alterations, which we will be examining in later chapters. Here then is the final proof of the antiquity of our roads. The primary layout was there by the time William the Conqueror arrived in England. It was perhaps centuries old by that time. All we have done since is to modify it slightly to meet with changing circumstances. It is to these we now turn.

# 4    Medieval Roads

From the Norman Conquest onwards we know much more about roads and tracks and our new knowledge comes from the numbers of historical documents which have survived from the medieval period. Sometimes these documents are obviously valuable for tracing roads. Perhaps the best known is the fourteenth-century Gough Map, which shows most of the major places in England and Wales, and from it we can deduce the main pattern of communications at that time. At a local level there are many manorial documents, especially those which relate to the offences brought before the manor courts which often mention highways and 'ways'. Thus in the 1461 court rolls for the Manor of Sawston, in Cambridgeshire, we read that 'John Webbe, *clericus* Paid 12d rent for A tennement next to a messuage called *Sarsayneshed* which abutted on the highway from Cambridge to Walden' and that John Durarnte paid 8d for 'two tofts each 20 feet wide, one of them abutting on Mellelane'. From these and from many other documents the whole medieval road system of the parish of Sawston can be established.

Many national records, kept by the developing medieval civil service, in the process of explaining the matters of justice or administration with which they were concerned give details of roads and lanes. In the *Curia Regis Rolls* for 1241, for example, which are a record of judicial cases heard by the King's Court, there are details of a dispute between two landowners. In the evidence is mention of a 'way' from the land of a place called Philipston, in Dorset, running towards a wood called Suthden. We know that Suthden is the present Sutton Holmes Plantation in the parish of Wimborne St Giles, but Philipston is a village which no longer exists. With the knowledge gained from this document and others we can not only find the site of the former village, but also identify the 'way' from it to the wood. This is a green lane, still in part a public footpath, but now

111

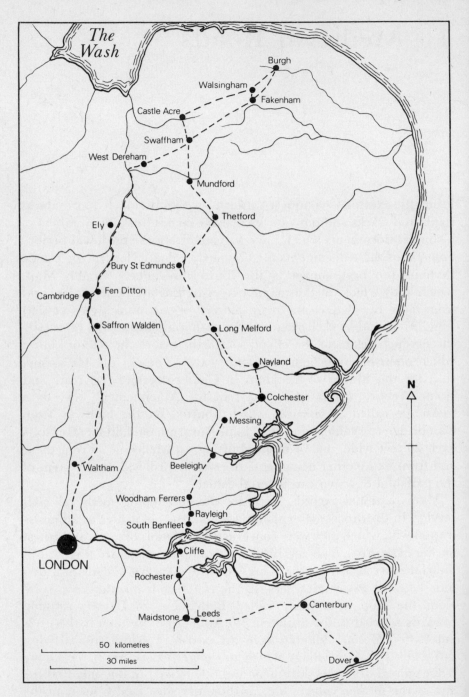

**Fig. 48 Route taken by Edward I, 1289–90**

hardly used. Yet in the thirteenth century it was the main track from Philipston village, through its fields, to the woodland pastures beyond. Though here a document shows that a medieval road has lost its former importance, others indicate, though not in a direct manner, the fact that many medieval roads are still used today. In medieval times the village of Silverstone in southern Northampton-shire was an important royal manor. There the king had a set of large fish ponds which had to be kept in good order. A series of thirteenth-century documents show what was involved in these works for they contain specific instructions from the king to carry out cer-tain tasks. These include sending to Oxford for nets to catch fish and dispatching the fish to the king's palace at Woodstock near Oxford. From this and other evidence it is possible to deduce that the medieval way between Silverstone and Oxford is the present main A43 trunk road via Brackley, while the road to Woodstock branched off this road through Kirtlington along the modern A4095 road. Both these have been much altered in detail since medieval times, and in particular the fine straight run of the A43 north of Oxford is the result of a massive road improvement scheme of the 1930s. Never-theless the general route in medieval times was the same as it is today.

Another method of tracing medieval roads is to examine royal letters and writs, constantly issued by the kings of England as they moved around the countryside, and to note the dates and places at which they were signed. Often a king would spend a few days at an abbey, then move to a convenient royal manor, and subsequently pass on to the home of a great magnate. At each stopping place the king would send off various orders as part of his administrative and judicial duties. By plotting these places on a map it is possible to see, fairly accurately, which were the major roads in use at that time. In most cases, either the roads still exist as main roads, or they are clearly traceable, but have declined in importance since. It is very rare to find that a documented medieval road has disappeared with-out trace. Almost invariably it has lost its original importance and changed its role, but it is nearly always there in some form today.

Perhaps the best king to produce this kind of evidence was Edward I, for he was a prodigious traveller. If we look at what he did in a few months in 1289–90 we can see where many of the main routes of medieval England were located (Fig. 48). In early August 1289 the king landed at Dover and commenced a pilgrimage to the shrines of well-known saints. He began by moving directly to Canterbury, presumably along the old Roman road which linked the two places and which is the modern A2. He then travelled west across the North Downs to the manor of Leeds near Maidstone. Here it is possible that the king and his retinue followed the old Pilgrims' Way south-east above the River Stour and then, north of Ashford, turned north-west and kept to the edge of the high ground, still along the Pilgrims' Way, to Hollingbourne where he would have descended to Leeds. If this is so, then we can certainly trace his way along the tracks and green lanes that exist here. On the other hand it is equally possible that the king took the more direct route, followed today by the A252 to Charing and thence along the modern A20 at the foot of the North Downs.

From Leeds the king travelled west into Maidstone where he joined the Roman road running north. This he followed, crossing the River Medway at Rochester, and then continued north along what is now a minor B-class road to the village of Cliffe on the Thames Estuary. From here he was carried by boat across the river to South Benfleet whence it is a short distance to his next stopping place, the great castle at Rayleigh in Essex. His next halt was at the abbey of Woodham Ferrers only five miles away and he probably travelled north along what are now winding country lanes to cross the River Crouch on the ferry at Hullbridge and thence on to Woodham. From here he moved a few more miles to Beeleigh Abbey on the outskirts of Maldon, following the present main road between Woodham and Maldon. The next stop was at the village of Messing near Tiptree, an easy ten-mile journey along a route followed today by the main Maldon to Colchester road. Beyond Messing the king continued to Colchester and then took the road north to Nayland which is the present A134. After a short break there he continued north-west via Sudbury to Long Melford and then to the great abbey at Bury St Edmunds along the route which the A134 still follows. From Bury the royal party struck out across the Breckland to Thetford in Norfolk and the same modern A134 marks their course. Beyond Thetford the modern road continues across the Breckland to the village of Mundford where the king crossed the River Wissey. He then travelled on northwards, through Swaffham as far as Castle Acre, along what is now the A1065, on north-east to Fakenham and down the valley of the little River Stiffkey to the great medieval shrine at Walsingham. After a short diversion east to Burgh, near Melton Constable, along what are now country lanes, the king commenced the journey to London. He first took what is now the main Cromer to Swaffham road, after which he turned south-west to West Dereham Abbey, near Downham Market.

At this point the king was on the edge of the fens and roads across them, though they existed, were often impassable. He thus boarded a boat at Downham, travelled along the Ouse to Ely, where he stayed at the abbey, and then continued south along the River Cam to Fen Ditton near Cambridge, where he lodged in the Bishop of Ely's palace. He then rode into Cambridge and set off south along the present A130 road until he met the main London to Norwich road near Saffron Walden. From there he moved down to Waltham Abbey and thence home to Westminster, along what is now the A11.

This long and apparently tedious journey was completed in exactly two months along roads which, although no doubt very different in appearance from those of today, are nevertheless all there and, for the most part, still in use. How different these medieval roads were can be seen by following part of another journey of Edward I, taken after the death of his beloved wife Eleanor on 25 November 1290, when he followed her bier from Harby near Lincoln, to Westminster. Edward marked the resting places of the cortege by erecting the well-known Eleanor Crosses. Two of the best that remain are those at Geddington, Northamptonshire, where the party stayed overnight at the royal palace, and at Delapre Abbey on the outskirts of Northampton, which the cortege reached the following day. Before arriving at Geddington the party had stayed at Stamford, though there the cross does not survive. Clearly the route taken from Stamford, via Geddington, to Northampton was along the present A43 and thus we can be sure that in the late thirteenth century this road was one of the major routes of England. Yet of course we can hardly expect the line of the modern road, which is a finely engineered trunk route, to be indentical to the medieval one in every respect. Over the succeeding centuries a number of minor and in some cases quite extensive changes have been made to it. We can look briefly at some of these to indicate the type of alteration that took place not only on this road, but on all roads over the course of time (Fig. 49).

For the first three miles from Stamford, as far as the village of Easton on the Hill, the modern and medieval roads are identical. Then at Easton the present road swings past the village on the line of a late eighteenth-century turnpike, cut to avoid a double bend in the main street. At Duddington a fine recently constructed bypass avoids the narrow medieval street of the village through which Queen Eleanor's body would have passed (Fig. 50). Beyond the bypass the modern and medieval roads rejoin and run on for another four miles to the village of Bulwick where they climb another narrow village street (Fig. 51). On the other side of the village the modern road becomes a straight, broad highway for just over a mile, hardly characteristic of a medieval one. To the west is the fine park of Bulwick House and there, preserved in the grassland, is the medieval road which was abandoned in the eighteenth century and replaced by the present one. Here we can see exactly what a main medieval route looked like on heavy clay land. It consists of a holloway over six feet deep, four feet wide across the bottom and some thirty-five feet across the top running obliquely down the valley side. Today it looks pleasant enough, covered with fine short turf, but in Edward's time it would have been extremely difficult to traverse, especially when wet weather turned the bottom into a quagmire and made it quite impossible for travellers actually to pass each other.

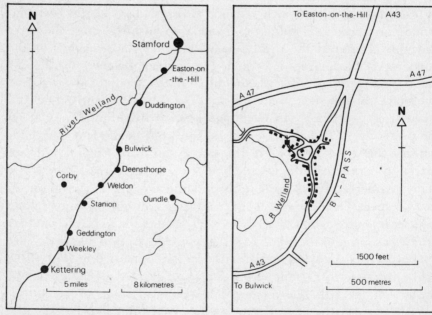

Fig. 49 Stamford-Kettering road, Northamptonshire
Fig. 50 Duddington, Northamptonshire

The medieval road can be traced either as a holloway or, where the slope steepens, as a narrow rutted terrace for over a mile until it meets the modern road again. For a hundred yards or so the two coincide, then the medieval road, now a narrow deeply cut lane, swings south through the tiny village of Deenethorpe, passes along the now dead-end main street and, as another holloway, crosses a marshy valley and climbs back to meet the modern road (Fig. 52). The latter taking the more direct route round Deenethorpe is a post-medieval improvement. Both old and new roads then run on together, though recent improvements have removed all the bends, for another two miles to the village of Weldon (Fig. 53). Here the medieval road ran through the village across a small stream on an ancient bridge. The present road, another post-medieval improvement, swings north of the village, crosses the stream higher up, and then bends south to meet the medieval route as it leaves the original village high street.

Again both routes run together for another two miles until the village of Stanion is reached (Fig. 54). Here the medieval road

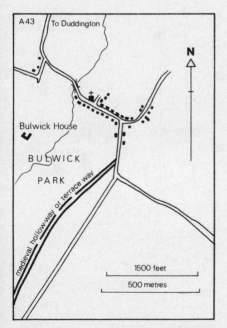
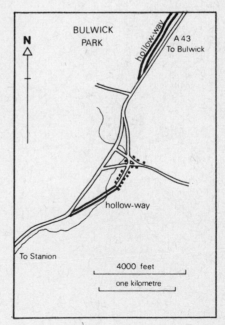

Fig. 51 Bulwick, Northamptonshire
Fig. 52 Deenethorpe, Northamptonshire

turned into the village, passed through a series of right-angled bends, along the main street and out at its southern end. Though this route caused no problems in medieval times, or indeed later, in the late eighteenth century when traffic increased it became totally inadequate. Thus a short bypass to the west of the village was built in 1790 when the road was turnpiked. After Stanion again both medieval and modern roads continue together for three miles to Geddington (Fig. 55). Now the present A43 passes west of the village on a well-made 1930s bypass, crossing the River Ise on a broad rein-forced concrete bridge; the medieval road, however, turned sharply east into the village and it was here, in the royal palace near the church, that Queen Eleanor's body rested for a night. The next morning the cortege passed down the main street of the village and crossed the River Ise at a ford (though in later times a fine, surviving medieval bridge replaced it). Beyond the village the modern bypass runs back onto the medieval route taken by the queen.

A mile beyond, the present A43 swings west in a broad curve and passes through the south-western corner of the village of Weekley

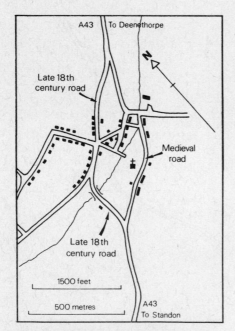

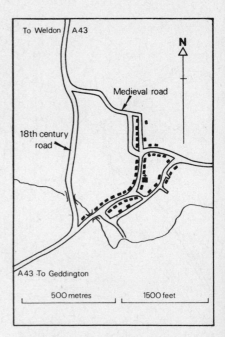

Fig. 53 Weldon, Northamptonshire
Fig. 54 Stanion, Northamptonshire

(Fig. 56) – but this was not the medieval route. The latter ran straight on into the centre of Weekley, past the church, and out on the other side. The diversion of the road to the west was carried out in 1716 when the Montagu family, who owned Boughton House to the east, started to expand their small estate into the huge landscaped park which exists today. The Montagus moved the existing road so that it followed the edge of the park, and today we can still see the medieval road running across the park as a holloway. Here it is somewhat more impressive then that of Bulwick, for it is up to thirty yards across and three to five feet deep. Though certainly this was wide enough for traffic to pass, in wet weather it would hardly have given an easy journey. Beyond Weekley the medieval and modern roads again meet and run down into the town of Kettering. This long description of some twenty-four miles of medieval track and modern trunk road has been given, not because it is especially remarkable, but because it is absolutely typical of thousands of miles of road in Britain. Most medieval main routes are still in existence in one form or another, often with very little alteration except in detail.

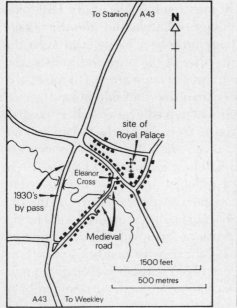
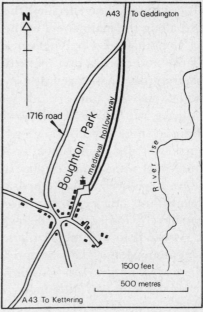

Fig. 55 Geddington, Northamptonshire
Fig. 56 Weekley, Northamptonshire

Sometimes the situation is more complex than the examples given above, in that on occasions there was more than one route which could be used and, while all can be considered as medieval, even during these centuries changes in importance and use occurred. A fine instance of this is the main route from London to the north as it crosses the old county of Huntingdonshire, now Cambridgeshire (Fig. 57). In the Roman period the road was the Ermine Street, which ran north-west from the Roman town of Godmanchester until it reached the high ground at Alconbury Hill. Here the road alignment was turned north and ran almost exactly straight for about ten miles, skirting the fens, until it reached high ground again. There it turned once more and ran straight for another four miles, passing through the now abandoned Roman town of Durobrivae, near Water Newton, where it crossed the River Nene on a bridge.

At the end of Roman times the section of this road between Alconbury Hill and the River Nene fell into disuse. The reasons for this are not clear but were perhaps the result of the collapse of the bridge across the Nene and the breaking up of the culverts which carried a multitude of streams under the road into the fens. Long-distance traffic began to take a new route to the west on higher, but drier ground. Travellers left the Roman road at Alconbury Hill, passed along the main street of the village of Upton and into the village of Coppingford. Coppingford village no longer exists, and even the banks and ditches that marked the sites of the medieval houses and their gardens have been destroyed, but the main street, an unusually wide holloway, and certainly wider than that found in most deserted villages, can still be seen, showing where medieval travellers passed. Beyond the site of Coppingford an old footpath marks the line of this medieval road, and thereafter for seven-and-a-half miles green lanes and quiet wandering country roads follow its course. In places these lanes have been straightened and widened, mainly in the late eighteenth and nineteenth centuries as part of the enclosure of the old medieval fields (see p.171 below), but basically it remains the old road.

At one point the modern lane passes a farm with the odd name of Ongutein Manor. This has great significance for just below the farm there was, until it was wantonly destroyed without warning, a small moated site. It was little more than a square island, surrounded by a broad water-filled ditch, but it was the site of a medieval manor house called Ogerston. The importance of this apparently minor place is that it is actually marked on the great Gough Map of Eng-

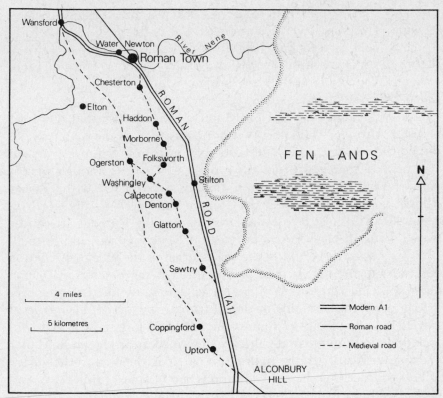

Fig. 57 Roman and medieval roads between Alconbury and Wansford, Cambridgeshire

land and Wales made in 1360. As all the places on that map appear to lie on main roads, the existence of Ogerston shows that at that period the lane which passes it today was the main road to the north. As it also went through the main street of Coppingford and Upton, which had probably existed in that form for three centuries, we are able to establish a period of long usage for this route.

To the north of Ogerston, a modern lane still marks the course of the medieval road for two-and-a-half miles. Afterwards it is lost, except for an old footpath, until the modern B-class road between Wansford and Elton is reached. From there the modern road and the medieval one are the same and they run directly into the main street of Wansford where they cross the River Nene. The name of the village suggests that there was once a ford across the river here, probably the first upstream from the broken Roman bridge at Water Newton. This may have been one reason why the medieval successor to the Roman road took the slightly longer and infinitely more wandering route to the west beyond Alconbury. In later times this ford was replaced by a magnificent bridge, which still survives and is dated 1577.

However, though we can prove fairly satisfactorily that this road between Alconbury Hill and Wansford was used as the main road to the north in both the eleventh and the fourteenth centuries, we can also be sure that it was not the only one. There is another almost parallel route, between the one already described and the earlier Roman road, which leaves the Roman road well to the north of Alconbury Hill, just before the later reaches the fen edge. It can be traced going through the main street of Sawtry village and through what was in medieval times the main street of the village of Glatton two miles further on. It then passed through the hamlets of Denton and Caldecote and into Washingley village, now, like Coppingford, utterly deserted. Here this medieval trunk road forked, for medieval travellers had a choice of routes: the left hand fork, now a footpath, took them back to the route already described, near Ogerston Manor and so into Wansford; the right hand one took them on to the village of Folksworth. From here a continuous run of lanes, bridle ways and footpaths through the villages of Morborne and Haddon to Chesterton mark the medieval road. At Chesterton the edge of the River Nene was reached, so the travellers turned north-west and moved along the edge of the river, via Water Newton, to reach the crossing place of the Nene at Wansford. This section today is traversed by the A1, now a dual carriageway motor road.

We have no direct evidence of the time in the medieval period when this road was in use. As it coincides with the main streets of a number of villages, it appears to have been an early one. On the other hand, when it reaches Wansford it approaches the latter village in a very awkward way involving two right-angled bends in order to cross the bridge. As the first road described runs directly into Wansford by a much easier route, this is likely to be the earlier of the two. However, whichever was the first, both were certainly used for much of the medieval period, and were probably of equal importance.

Yet there was a third route in medieval times across this region, the Roman road itself. For though, as we have seen, in early post-

Roman times it was probably abandoned in favour of the more westerly routes, there is no doubt that by the twelfth century most of it
was back in use. Only the extreme northern end, close to the original
Roman crossing of the River Nene, was permanently abandoned.
There the medieval road joined the one running north from Chesterton, skirted the river, and crossed it at Wansford with the other
routes. The evidence for the use of this road in medieval times is
clear on the ground today at the village of Stilton which lies across
its line.

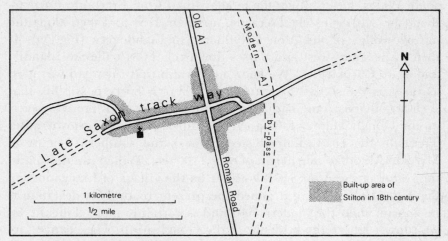

Fig. 58 Stilton, Cambridgeshire

If we look at Stilton village (Fig. 58) very carefully we can see that
the parish church is at the western end, quite remote from the
Roman road, and alongside an east to west street. It is obvious that
before the Roman road came back into use Stilton village had grown
up along an east to west trackway which was then the main one in the
area, so we may hazard a guess and say that in the ninth or tenth
century, or perhaps a little earlier, when Stilton was developing into
a village, the Roman road was not important. However, as traffic
developed along the latter it tended to alter the shape of Stilton.
Growth of the village came to be concentrated along the newly
developing north to south road, not the original east to west one,
presumably in response to the commercial advantages to be gained
by building inns or shops on the new main road.

Thus, in the final analysis, we can see that throughout medieval times there were three separate, but roughly parallel, main roads between London and the north in Huntingdonshire. At any time one may have been more important than the others, but all were in use and in fact remained so until well into the post-medieval period. Even in the eighteenth century, by which time the Roman road via Wansford had become the main one, long-distance cattle drovers still used the others.

Once more this complex story of a few miles of main road is not unusual and can be paralleled in many places all over Britain. In south Wales, for example, the modern road from Brecon to Carmarthen (the A40) runs via Trecastle, up Cwm Dwr and then along the narrow valley of the Afon Gwydderig to Llandovery (Fig. 59). It then turns south-west and passes down the Tywi valley to Llandilo and on to Carmarthen. We know for certain that this road was used as early as the sixteenth century, and there is every possibility that such an obvious route had been used for centuries before. However, on the Gough Map of 1360 a slightly different route is shown. After Trecastle the road climbed steeply over the southern heights of Mynydd Myddfau to a height of over 1100 feet. It then ran down into the valley of the Afon Sawdde as far as the village of Llangadock in the Tywi Valley where it joined the present road. This deviation is no shorter than the modern A40 and is certainly more difficult, yet we cannot ignore the evidence of the Gough Map. The chances are that both roads were in use in the medieval period, and that in the

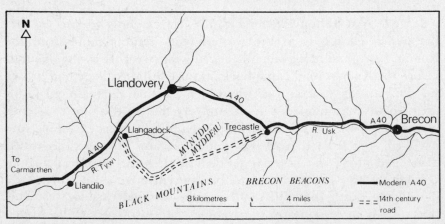

Fig. 59 Medieval and modern roads, Brecon, Carmarthen

fourteenth century, the upland road was then the one in fashion. Incidentally this upland road is still in existence as a metalled lane throughout its whole length.

In eastern England the medieval road from London to Norwich shows the same pattern of multiple routes where it crosses the Breckland. The present A11 road between Newmarket and Thetford, bridging the River Lark at Barton Mills, is a fine modern highway and it has been a main road for centuries. There were at least two other alternative routes further south-east in medieval times, one via Herringswell and Tuddenham, crossing the Lark at Temple Bridge, and the other which forded the river at Lackford. Both these routes still exist, though for most of their length they are now only bridle ways. The track across Cavenham Heath (Plate VI) is a well-known place for Sunday walkers and it is difficult to believe that it was once a major road.

A particularly important point in the development of these medieval roads is that they often changed the shape of the villages through which or near which they passed. As we saw above, the village of Stilton actually altered its shape in response to the changing pattern of communications within the area, which illustrates the most important aspect of medieval roads, that the growth and decline of various parts of the medieval road system of Britain, whether nationally or locally, can be seen and understood in the landscape itself.

We saw in the last chapter how the layout of the first villages was usually conditioned by the route pattern that existed at that time. Thus a village would become strung out along a main road or it would take on a cross-shaped plan if it grew up at a point where two existing roads intersected. However, villages did not remain static: they grew or shrank in response to population changes and, most important from our point of view, they reacted to changes in communication patterns. The example of Stilton quoted above illustrates the sequence of events that could take place almost anywhere. At a rough guess at least half of all the medieval villages in Britain will show some alteration of their basic plans as a result of variations in the importance of their local road systems. Many of these alterations have taken place in recent centuries but others occurred in the medieval period. However it is not easy to recognize how a village has changed. It often requires a great deal of specialized knowledge and hard work to be sure of producing the correct answer, but it is worthwhile, for the results are of considerable interest and much more satisfying then glib assumptions about 'medieval ways' that pepper the local history scene.

A splendid example of this kind of village movement, largely because it can be partly dated, is Grantchester just outside Cambridge (Fig. 60). The village has a curious plan which has puzzled historians for years, yet in fact it is relatively simply to explain. The Saxon village grew up along on old road leading down to a ford across the River Cam, on what was then the main east to west routeway across the area. Part of the road down to the Cam is now a disused holloway, but there is still a footpath along its line to show that it has never been quite abandoned. In later centuries a watermill was built further upstream and part of the work there involved the construction of a huge dam across the river in order to pond back water to drive the mill wheels. This dam provided a much easier crossing than the old ford, and was in a more convenient place to reach the next village of Trumpington. As a result the old road to the ford fell into disuse and a new road was developed from the village centre to the mill dam, but by that time the area to the south of the village was occupied by rectangular blocks of strips of the medieval common fields. The new road could not, therefore, run directly to the mill but was forced around the edges of the fields, following the access ways through them, and thus took on its present appearance of numerous right-angled bends, becoming established as the main route out of the village in this direction. Then, as the population of Grantchester expanded, there was 'ribbon development' along this new road. Gradually houses were erected on the former village fields and Grantchester took on a new shape. The most interesting feature of this development is that it appears to have taken place at a very early date in the medieval period. One of the buildings along this new road is the parish church which, though mainly of late medieval date, has some twelfth-century work in it, so we can be sure that the village had already moved onto its new road by that time at the latest.

Grantchester may be more complex than usual but most villages show a simple reaction to a change in the importance of local roads. Probably more typical is Gilmorton, in south Leicestershire, which today has a basic L-shaped plan arranged along two arms of a cross roads. Careful study of the village shows that it originated, perhaps in late Saxon times, along the then main road of the area which ran

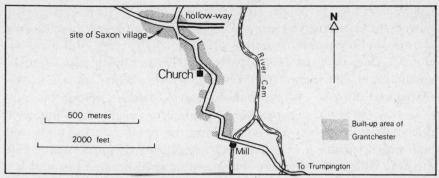

Fig. 60 Grantchester, Cambridgeshire

north-west to south-east. The church, manor house and most of the houses lay along this route, but later in the medieval period the north-east to south-west road either became more important or was of equal importance. As a result the normal expansion of the village took place along the south-western road, so producing the present plan.

In some villages the sequence of development is not so easy to understand. This is because, instead of straightforward continual expansion from the original layout along the new road system, many villages actually moved from their old site to a new one. The evidence for this movement can sometimes be found in documents, but more often it is revealed in abandoned streets and house sites. An instance of this is Knapwell in Cambridgeshire (Fig. 61). Today the

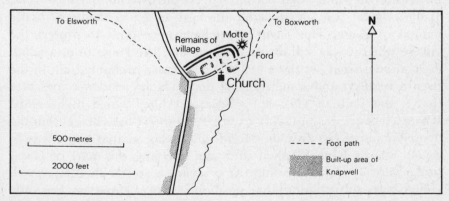

Fig. 61 Knapwell, Cambridgeshire

village is strung out along a north to south lane which is the main, indeed the only, road across the parish, but if we look carefully we can see that the parish church is isolated from the rest of the village, along a lane, now only a footpath, which runs north-east from the north end of the village street. On either side of this lane are banks, scarps and ditches of former houses, together with a system of abandoned lanes, which suggests that at some time in the early medieval period the village was arranged along the north-east to south-west lane which led down to a ford and which indeed can be traced into the next village of Boxworth. Then as this road became less and less important Knapwell gradually moved through a right angle to the increasingly important north to south road. Why this move took place is not clear. Certainly we have no written evidence for it and thus can only guess the reasons. One possible one is that Knapwell was originally a daughter hamlet of an earlier village of Elsworth to the west. That is, it was set up in a corner of the land of Elsworth, perhaps in late Saxon times. At that time the main route from Elsworth to Boxworth ran east to west across the ford at this point. Thus Knapwell presumably grew up along this road but, as the years rolled by, it became an independent settlement with its own fields, and eventually a parish. As its fields all lay to the south of the new village, the Knapwell farmers would have tended to use the north to south track to reach them, so this route became the locally more important one, and the village moved from its original position on the old track to the more convenient one.

We do not know the date of this change. Unlike Grantchester the church here cannot help us, but there is a little evidence to indicate a time when the village had not moved. At the extreme north-east end of the original lane, overlooking the ford, is a tiny medieval castle mound or motte. This castle must have been built to protect the village when it was still on its original site. We know from a small excavation carried out there in 1929 that it was probably built in the twelfth century, and some indirect documentary evidence indicates that it was built in 1142–3 by Ramsey Abbey which then owned Knapwell. This was probably in order to protect the village from the depredations of Geoffrey de Mandeville, who, at that time, was in revolt against King Stephen and was harrying this part of Cambridgeshire. If we are reading the evidence correctly then Knapwell village was still in its original position in 1142. However, certainly by the early seventeenth century, the village was in its present position as a number of the standing houses are of that date. We cannot achieve a closer dating than this, but it does appear that Knapwell moved its position completely some time in the late medieval period in response to the changing local road pattern.

Sometimes there was a more radical change in the importance of a road pattern which altered the shape of a village. Only a few miles from Knapwell is the village of Caxton (Fig. 62). It lies along the Roman Ermine Street from London to the north and consists of little more than a row of houses on each side of that road. As at Knapwell the present church is not in the village, but in Caxton's case the church is some distance away, almost completely isolated. Examination of the land around the church has led to the discovery of abandoned lanes and holloways, some banks and ditches indicating former houses, and a large quantity of medieval pottery dating from the eleventh to the thirteenth centuries. This evidence shows that in these years the village lay around its church in the normal way. But by the early thirteenth century the old Roman road had become the Great North Road leading from London to Huntingdon, Stamford and Lincoln. Much traffic was moving along the road and the lord of

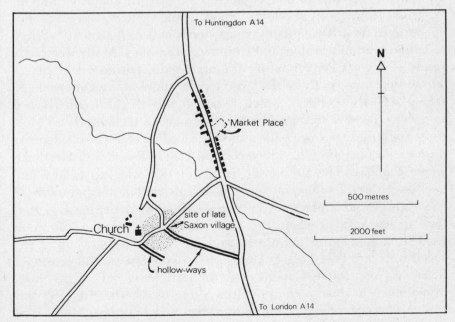

Fig. 62 Caxton, Cambridgeshire

the manor of Caxton, one Baldwin de Freville, probably looked long-
ingly at this traffic and no doubt wondered how he could exploit it.
And exploit it he did, for in 1247 he obtained permission from the
king to hold a weekly market in Caxton. Now a market in the village
as it was then would have been of little advantage to de Freville, so,
as far as we can see, he actually moved the village from around the
church to its new site on the Roman road. Here the new houses, set
in curving gardens based on the shape of the pre-existing strip fields,
were erected and a rectangular market place built in the centre of
this village at the top of a hill. In this more favourable position,
Caxton, and de Freville, were able to tap the commercial capacity of
the main road. Caxton became a minor market centre whose prosperity lasted right up until the eighteenth century when the Great
North Road moved to a new route further west, now the A1. Here,
once again, by looking at villages very carefully, the ebb and flow of
roads and road systems in the medieval period can be traced and
explained.

Towns, just as much as villages, also reflect the history of
medieval roads and tracks. Towns as we known them started to
appear towards the end of the late Saxon period. As a result of modern scholarship, we can now be fairly sure that the majority of them,
far from growing up slowly at 'good' route centres, were actually
encouraged as urban units by kings, lords and bishops for a variety
of military, administrative and commercial reasons. Many were, as a
result of a good eye for future financial gain, positioned at places
where the route centre of the time would allow urban expansion to
take place easily. Others, which were not so well sited, either failed
to develop or were strangled by later changes in the national or local
route pattern. One town which shows the effect of a well-chosen site
on routes which always remained important is Royston in Hertfordshire (Fig. 63). The site of the present town was, up to the late
twelfth century, literally an empty no man's land on the boundary of
two counties, at a place where five parishes met. Yet even at that
time it was an area where two important routes crossed, the main
road from London to the north, and the major routeway from the
south-west into East Anglia. Thus, when in the late twelfth century a
house of Augustinan Canons was founded here, one of the early
priors must have seen the potential value of the site. In 1189 this
priory obtained the right to hold a market and a fair here, and a new
town was laid out. Royston today still shows how this first plan was

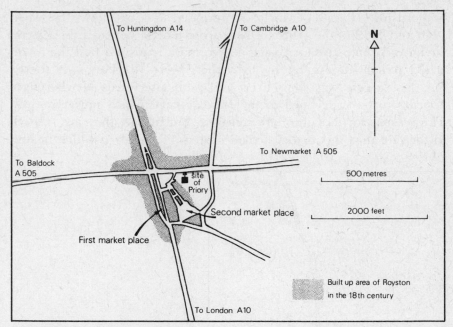

Fig. 63 Royston, Hertfordshire

made to fit the existing route pattern. The London road, because it was then the most important, was widened to produce a cigar-shaped market place on both sides of the cross roads, and plots for houses and shops were laid out alongside it. The town was immediately successful and grew rapidly: not only were other grants for a second fair obtained in 1213 and a third one in 1243, but permanent shops were built over the original market place to such an extent that a second market place had to be added at one side.

Other towns which show the same kind of success story are Newmarket in Suffolk, which is basically a simple wide main street along the London to Norwich Road, and Honiton in Devon which is of similar form on the London to Exeter Road. Both are late foundations, Newmarket of 1217–23 and Honiton 1194–1217, but there are many similar examples all over Britain which reflect the same success story.

There are also the towns that failed, however, and of these a large number did so because they were not related to a good route system, or because that system changed. One is the village of Newborough in

Staffordshire (Fig. 64), which was founded as a new town between 1100 and 1139 in the centre of Needwood Forest between the Rivers Trent and Dove at the crossing of two main roads. At first the town was a minor success, for by 1313 there were 101 burgesses there, but this success was short lived and soon afterwards Newborough appears to have declined to the small village which now remains. The reasons for its failure are complex, but in part they are related to the fact that the medieval road system of the area, which is still

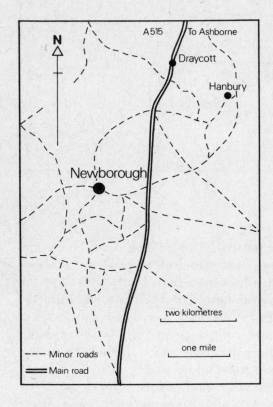

Fig. 64 Newborough, Staffordshire

there, did not retain its former importance and other routes developed leaving Newborough out on a limb. An even worse failure was that of Hindon in Wiltshire, which was founded by the Bishop of Winchester in 1220, in a corner of his manor of East Knoyle at the junction of a group of relatively minor roads (Fig. 65). None of these routes ever became important and the 'town' remained a village even though it sent representatives to parliament until 1832.

Nevertheless many towns could and did adapt themselves to the

fluctuating importance of roads, provided that there was a firm base
to build their success upon. One such is Hungerford, in Berkshire.
The town grew up between 1086 and 1131, along what must have
been at that time the main road of the area, a north to south route
between Oxford and the south. As a result Hungerford was laid out
as a single street running up the steep side of the Kennet Valley. But
by the fourteenth century at the latest the previous minor road along
the side of the river at the bottom of the town had become part of the

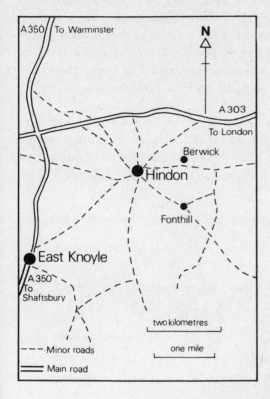

Fig. 65 Hindon, Wiltshire

main route from London to Bath. As a result, though it still retained
its original form along the north to south road, Hungerford
expanded along the later road, joining the village of Eddington and
ultimately giving it a basic T-shaped plan which can still be seen
today.

Hungerford had a relatively easy task in adapting to a new road,
while towns such as Royston and Newmarket never had the need.
Hindon failed because the roads did not become important. But at

many places the existing road systems were deliberately altered, either when the town was established or later on to enable it to survive. A town which appears to have had the pre-existing road system altered to suit it is Bicester in Oxfordshire. The town was laid out on a major north to south road, now the A41 Banbury to Aylesbury road, and grew up along it. But an equally important route, the old Towcester to Alcester Roman Road running north-east to south-west, passed the town at its northern end. To avoid loss of revenue by travellers bypassing Bicester, a short section of the Roman road was either abandoned or blocked and through traffic was diverted into the main north to south street, and then at the market place turned back along a narrow street to the Roman road again. Only in this century, when modern conditions threatened to choke the town, was the old Roman road line rebuilt and the town centre again bypassed.

Another example of roads being diverted to a town in order to ensure its success is to be found at St Ives in Huntingdonshire (Fig. 66). There, about 1110, the Abbot of Ramsey laid out a new town on the edge of the River Ouse, just outside the existing village

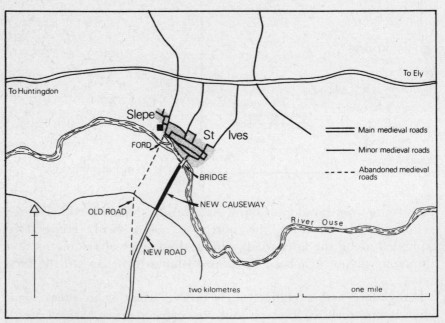

Fig. 66 St Ives, Cambridgeshire

of Slepe, well to the south of the main east to west road. There was also a north to south route in the vicinity but it crossed the river at a ford at Slepe, just upstream from the new town. In order to make sure that traffic came into the town, a new mile-long road was constructed on a huge causeway across the floodplain of the River Ouse and, crossing the river on a new bridge, entered the town in the centre of its market place. The fine medieval bridge, though not in fact the original one, as well as the causeway, still exist to show clearly what was done.

A town which had to overcome a similar problem was Lichfield in Staffordshire (Fig. 67). Although the ecclesiastical centre of Saxon Mercia and the site of a great cathedral, the town itself did not come into being until some time between 1129 and 1149 when it was deliberately founded by Bishop de Clinton and given a neat grid pattern of streets. However, though the pre-existing main north-east to south-west route passed through the new town, there was no way for the long-distance travellers going from London to the north-west to make use of the town. These people probably used the Roman road, the Watling Street, three miles to the south. Such travellers

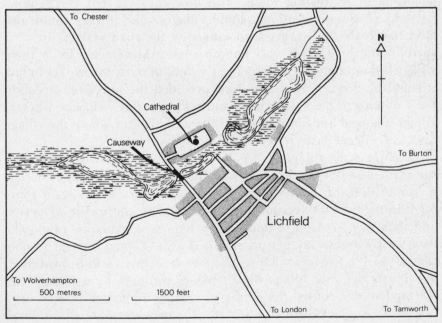

Fig. 67 Lichfield, Staffordshire

that actually came to the town from the south-east were faced with a long diversion to the north-east of over two miles merely to cross the water-filled and marshy valley which lay between the town and the road north-west to Chester and North Wales. Thus the town's prosperity was severely limited and it was not until 1296 when a later Bishop built a causeway across the valley that the town came into its own. The causeway provided a direct route through the town and, as a result, the old Roman road lost its former importance. The road via Lichfield became the major cross-country route. By the 1360s this road through Lichfield was the main route to the north-west, as the Gough Map shows. This importance lasted until the early nineteenth century when the Roman road was rebuilt as the London to Holyhead Road, and then Lichfield declined in status. Here we can see how the relatively minor work of constructing a causeway under 100 yards long across a valley not only led to the success of a new town but changed the relative importance of a national routeway. Almost all towns in Britain can, if looked at carefully and with understanding, show the various changes that took place in roads and trackways in the medieval period.

Though we have looked at villages and seen how their shapes were conditioned by existing roads, and how they reacted to changing patterns of communications, some villages, like towns, could also alter markedly the relative importance of the road systems in their surrounding area. This was not an easy achievement, for a mere village did not have the commercial weight of most towns, yet in fact it could be done, if a suitable lord provided the pressure, or conditions to make it possible. Two instances show this well, one where a village changed a major national route and another where the village altered the local pattern of communications.

The first is the village of Woolpit, in Suffolk, which used to lie on the main A45 Bury St Edmunds to Ipswich road (Fig. 68). There is no doubt that this modern major road has been an important route for centuries. It was certainly greatly used in the medieval period and there is no reason to doubt that, like most roads, its origins lie back in the prehistoric period. Yet it is also of some interest to note that along the fourteen-mile section between Bury and Stowmarket, Woolpit is the only village that it passes through. Everywhere else, the modern and indeed the medieval villages lie just off it. And originally the road avoided Woolpit too, for its older line, still a small minor lane, can be traced running in a broad curve well to the north

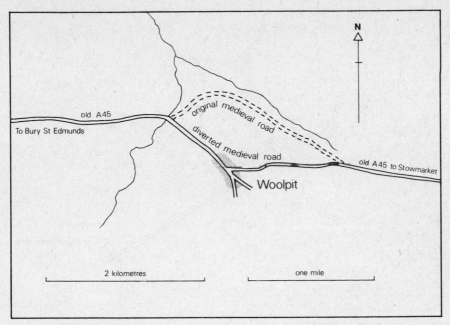

Fig. 68 Woolpit, Suffolk

of the village. The modern road swings off the old road at a sharp
angle north-west of Woolpit, and then turns sharply east in the
centre of the village when it reaches the old east to west main street.
Thus the modern road looks as if it has been deliberately altered to
pass through Woolpit. This is perhaps the correct explanation, for
we know that in the thirteenth century Woolpit was granted a
weekly market and an annual fair in an attempt to make it a local
centre of some importance. This succeeded to some degree and, as a
result, the main road was either deliberately changed to pass
through the village or gradually moved from its old route to the later
one. It is not without interest to note that in recent years, when the
A45 became a major road for container traffic between Felixstowe
docks and the Midlands, the medieval road through Woolpit had to
be abandoned. A new bypass has been cut around the north side of
the village, running almost parallel to the original early medieval
through road.

A much more complex example, this time involving more local
routes, is the village of Long Buckby, in Northamptonshire (Fig. 69).
As far as we can see, the original late Saxon village lay south-west of

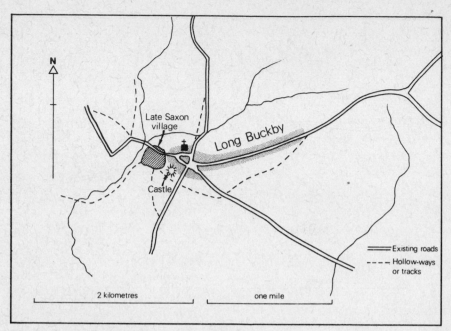

Fig. 69 Long Buckby, Northamptonshire

the modern one, on the side of the valley of a small brook. The
village was still there in the twelfth century when a large motte and
bailey castle was built on the high land above it in a protective situation. Some of the roads into this late Saxon village still exist, though
they are no longer true roads. From the east and south-east a continuous line of footpaths marks the way into the Saxon village, and
more definite proof of the great age of these paths is the existence of
long sections of deeply cut holloway along their line. The road west
from the original village is also there today as a track, lying in the
bottom of a great holloway as it runs down the valley side. The track
then takes the form of a terrace swinging south-west along the
stream. The existing road into the present village from the north
also seems to have led into the old Saxon village.

Then, in 1280, Henry de Lacy, Earl of Lincoln and later Earl of
Salisbury, obtained the grant of a weekly market and two annual
fairs for his manor of Buckby. Apparently the old village was not
considered suitable for the commercial activity which he hoped
would come from the market and fairs, so a completely new village
was laid out north-east of the old one. It was given a neat rectangu-

lar market place and a new church, both of which still exist. The new village was clearly a success, for the old village declined to a few houses and a collection of abandoned house sites, while its successor grew larger and larger along a completely different road system to such an extent that it changed it name to *Long* Buckby.

The old roads also fell into disuse and new tracks from the north-west, north-east, south-east and south-west all developed, leading into the new village. Yet it must be recognized that these roads were new for only a relatively short distance beyond the village. Within a mile and a half at the most they all returned to the much older road system of the area. Here once again we see the recurring feature of all roads and tracks – the minor modification through time of basic routes, established in the very remote past.

So far in this examination of medieval roads, we have concentrated our attention on major routeways and the more important local tracks, but these were only a very small proportion of the sum total of trackways which surrounded every village and hamlet. All rural settlements in every part of Britain possessed a complex system of tracks which led, not only from one village to the next or from one village to a town, but from the village to its fields, its pastures, wastes, meadows and woodland. They were used mainly for agricultural purposes and their history and details are little known. Nevertheless they formed an important part of the totality of medieval roads and tracks and they cannot be ignored.

There were basically three kinds of track within this overall category of rural roads. By the medieval period, most villages in southern and midland England, and in a few other places in the north-east and north-west, had acquired a common field system made up of great numbers of strips grouped into blocks or furlongs. Numerous unfenced trackways gave access to these strips, usually running along the headlands between them. In woodland areas, such as the great forests of Sherwood, Needwood and Wychwood in the Midlands, on the moorland edges of south-western and northern England and on the lower mountain slopes of Wales and Scotland, where the land had been divided up into hedged or stonewalled fields as the wastes had been reclaimed, there were also countless wandering lanes which enabled farmers to reach these fields, or pass through them to the upland pastures. Lastly, on the mountains or moorlands themselves, as well as on the unreclaimed fenlands and coastal marshes, there were also unfenced tracks or drove roads along which the seasonal movement of animal herds took place or where villagers and farmers trekked for bracken, peat, fish or other necessities of life freely available to them in these marginal areas. Some of these latter tracks also had specialized uses connected both with industry and warfare.

The trackways or access roads of the open or common field systems of England seem the rarest of all roads of whatever date. Unlike most prehistoric tracks and Roman roads they have not always survived as routes into the present day. This is because in postmedieval times and especially in the eighteenth and early nineteenth centuries when these common fields were swept away and replaced by the hedged fields which are the familiar pattern we have now, these access roads disappeared with them. Yet it would be a grave mistake to think that we can no longer see them, for the majority survive in various forms. In a very few places, as a result of accidents of history, the actual medieval strip fields still remain today, although much modified in detail. Examples may be seen at Braunton in Devon, on the Isle of Portland in Dorset, at Laxton in Nottinghamshire, Soham in Cambridgeshire and Rhossilli in South Wales. Here we can still see the regular blocks of long, narrow strips, unencumbered by hedges or walls, and often still cultivated in a medieval fashion. And along the ends of each block of strips are broad open headlands, which were, and are, the places where the plough turned after completing each run along the strips. Many, but not all, of these headlands were also ploughed when the ploughing of the strips themselves was completed. But before that process took place, and especially in the case of the headlands that were never ploughed, they were used by the farmers to gain access to the strips themselves. Thus today we can go to Laxton, for example, and still walk along these wide grassy headlands between the cultivated strips and see modern farmers using them in the same way as their medieval predecessors.

However, over the greater part of England such strip or common fields no longer exist in use but their physical remains still lie across thousands of acres of the English landscape in the form of the ubiquitous ridge and furrow. This consists of long, rounded ridges, separated by furrows which, arranged in curving blocks, still cover much of the grasslands and indeed arable lands of lowland England. These ridges are not the actual strips themselves, for the individual strips in the medieval common fields were made up of groups of

these ridges, but they do reflect the general layout of the original
strips and, more particularly, the blocks of strips or furlongs. If we
look carefully at this ridge and furrow, two types of track can be
seen. First there are the local tracks leading from one village to
another through the ridge and furrow. These are often holloways
which can sometimes be traced for long distances across the countryside (Fig. 70). The other type of track is perhaps not so obvious at
first sight. At the ends of many blocks of ridge and furrow we can
often see the original headlands on which the plough was turned.
Sometimes they are just ridges set at right angles to the strips and
ploughed after them. Others are more complex, sometimes with the
adjacent ridges riding up onto them leaving a lower, slightly hollowed, central valley which was always an unploughed access way,
or often just a broad area separating two adjacent blocks of ridges.
These were the permanent access ways which were never ploughed
(Fig. 71). In any area of Midland England where there is permanent
pasture, and especially in parts of Buckinghamshire, Northamptonshire, Warwickshire or Leicestershire, one can still see quite clearly
these two kinds of tracks.

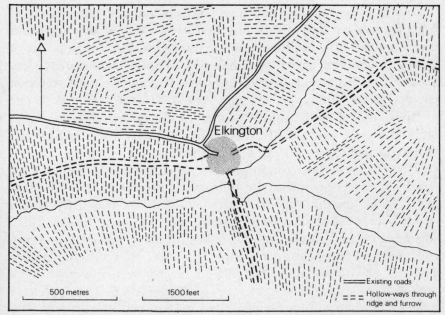

Fig. 70 Medieval fields and tracks, Elkington, Northamptonshire

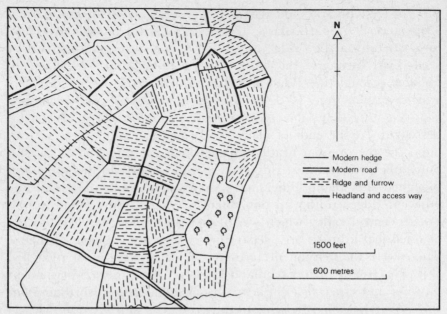

Fig. 71 Access ways in ridge and furrow, Stanford, Northamptonshire

Even in these regions, however, and certainly in other parts of England, modern agriculture has destroyed most of the ridge and furrow and left little but huge open arable fields. But all the power of large-scale modern agriculture has not completely removed every trace of these fields and their access ways. Among the most common features of the landscape, though very difficult to see unless one becomes attuned to the minor aspects of the countryside, are long, low ridges some ten to thirty yards wide and only a few inches high which run, sometimes for hundreds of yards.

If the crop and light conditions are good, one can sometimes see parallel lines of three, four or more such ridges, up to 200 yards apart. These are the original headlands of the medieval fields and are all that is left of the complex pattern of ridge and furrow. Such ridges can be seen all over the Midlands, in many places in southern England, and there are some fine examples in northern Norfolk (Fig. 72). Of course, as we have already noted, such ridges were not only headlands, but the access ways of the fields too. Thus when we have the total abandonment of a track system and its apparent destruction, the remains are still just visible in the modern landscape.

In a number of places these actual access roads still exist as tracks, albeit in a modified form. When the medieval open fields were enclosed in the eighteenth and nineteenth centuries some of the more important original access ways were kept in use. They were often altered out of all recognition, in that they were usually straightened and edged by neat hawthorn hedges, but they can still be recognized today, though it sometimes needs a little historical research to identify them. Such tracks exist in south-east Cambridgeshire. In medieval times when the long strip parishes there had their common fields on the lower land and the common pasture on the upper, higher parts, there had to be an access way through this arable land from the village to the upland pasture. A number of old estate maps survive which show these access ways wandering between the strips down the central axes of the parishes. When the common fields were swept away in the late eighteenth century and replaced by the modern hedged fields, it was still found necessary to have an axial parish road to enable farmers to reach their new enclosed fields, or to con-

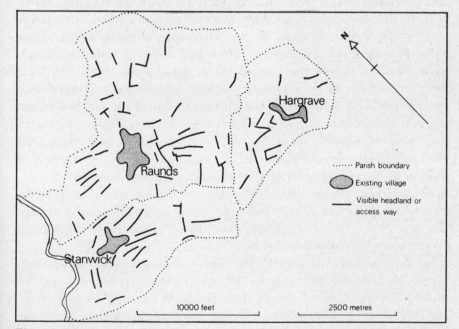

Fig. 72 Medieval headlands or access ways, Raunds, Stanwick and Hargrave, Northamptonshire

nect the new farmsteads which were built out in these fields. So the medieval tracks were retained, though they were often considerably altered and made exactly straight, usually thirty feet wide in the normal fashion of enclosure roads. All these roads still exist today, though as always they have changed their status and form over the years. Thus in four adjacent parishes in south-east Cambridgeshire, each of which has such an axial road, those at Little Wilbraham and Swaffham Bulbeck have become minor through roads to other villages, that at Swaffham Prior is a narrow strip of tarmac leading nowhere except to four farmsteads, while that at Bottisham is a long 'green' lane, much used by Sunday afternoon walkers (see Fig. 80).

In other places the medieval access roads have survived more nearly in their original form as a result of a different history. There the medieval common or strip fields did not last until the eighteenth or nineteenth centuries, then to be enclosed by Acts of Parliament, but were enclosed piecemeal over the centuries as a result of private agreements between various landowners. It was not an easy matter for one or two individuals to enclose their strips while their neighbours continued to farm in the old manner. Even after exchanges and purchases which consolidated scattered strips the resulting block of land, then in single ownership, was still surrounded by open strips and its shape was dictated by the curvature of these strips. Thus when this land was enclosed it often had curving hedges or stone walls which followed the line of the original strip edges. As time went on, whole areas of former strips were gradually divided into curved, enclosed fields and to reach these some of the old headlands or access ways were left as lanes between the new fields, often with their original winding form. Such lanes may still be seen today. At Hinton St Mary in central Dorset, for example, where a great deal of piecemeal enclosure took place in the sixteenth and seventeenth centuries, not only do the modern fields have a long curved strip form, but the lanes between them have the gentle sinuous line and abrupt changes of direction indicating that they were once the medieval access ways through open fields.

So far we have assumed that these common field ways were medieval in origin. But can we be sure of this? It depends on our understanding of the origins of these fields. We saw in the last chapter that there is now good evidence that the arrangement of the blocks of strips in the medieval common fields was probably based on Roman enclosed fields which had trackways running through them. If this idea is correct then many of these access ways in the medieval fields may have been used in Roman times and, as was suggested earlier, in that case they may well be of prehistoric origin. Once more we are faced with the situation seen so often already, that we are still using roads or tracks which are of the greatest antiquity and which have changed only slightly over thousands of years.

The second type of rural medieval road, that which lay in what might be termed the marginal regions of medieval Britain, includes those in the lands reclaimed from the forests, fens and moorlands. These roads are characterized by their winding nature, and by their boundaries of earthen banks in the forests, massive stone walls on the moorlands, or deep drainage ditches in the fens. All are tracks which were used by medieval farmers as they cleared forest, reclaimed moors or drained fenland and created out of such lands enclosed fields of various kinds.

On the lower slopes of all the upland areas of Britain one can still see the irregular pattern of stone-walled fields with winding lanes passing through them (Fig. 73). It is particularly well marked around the edges of Dartmoor and one often finds that the tracks

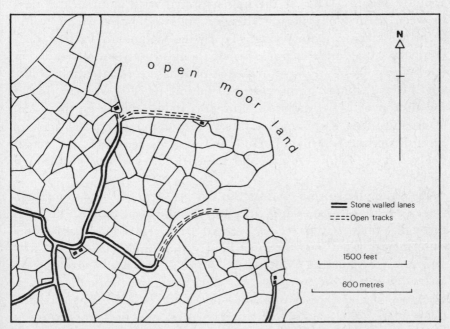

Fig. 73 Medieval moorland roads and tracks, Willsworthy, Devon

themselves are cut much lower than the surrounding fields. This is partly the result of natural wear and partly that farmers actually dug out the mud and rubbish that accumulated in these tracks and used it for manure on their fields. Even lanes now carefully tarmaced still show from their sunken nature the results of this medieval agricultural habit.

The same winding lanes occur in the areas once forested and here, especially where the former forests were in royal hands in the early medieval period, the dates of the clearance of the woodland and the establishment of the fields can be ascertained from the very good documentary record that describes the process. There is plenty of evidence in the medieval documents concerned with the royal forests of fines paid for illegal clearances, or assarting as it was known. Much of this assarting took place between the twelfth and fourteenth centuries when tens of thousands of acres of woodland were turned into farmland. In the village of Whiteparish, Wiltshire, for example, which lay on the edge of the Royal Forest of Melchet, we have records of fields being created from the woodland from the mid thirteenth century to the mid fourteenth century. In just one year, 1330, we know that nearly 75 acres of land were cleared; we can actually identify some of the fields formed at that time and pass between them along narrow, deeply hollowed lanes which would seem to be contemporary (Fig. 74). In the fenlands of eastern England, the same kinds of tracks exist, though in an entirely different landscape. Again we have evidence of massive reclamation of the edges of the fenland in the medieval period: in 1251 we read that in the Bishop of Ely's Manor of Littleport in the middle of the Cambridgeshire fens, sixty new tenants were holding about 500 acres of recently reclaimed fenland. Here too we can recognize the actual fields and still follow the irregular fen-edge lanes which run through them.

Yet again we run up against the old problem of the date of such tracks, for we cannot assume that they are the same date as the fields through which they pass. They could be much older tracks which were incorporated into the later field system and reused for a new purpose. Certainly at Whiteparish some of the roads through the forest fields can be proved to be older than the fields themselves. One, which gives access to some fields made in 1255, was certainly there nearly 200 years before when the area was still wooded for it leads to a farm which was in existence in 1086. Another, which

VIII   Medieval and later holloways cutting through Roman fields, Whiteparish, Wiltshire

IX   Medieval bridge, Braybrooke, Northamptonshire

X  The George Hotel,
   Huntingdon, a
   seventeenth-century and
   later coaching inn

XI  Milestone on the military
    road, Tomintoul, High-
    lands, Scotland

XII    An eighteenth-century moorland lane, Settle, Yorkshire

XIII    A nineteenth-century enclosure road, Wareham Heath, Dorset

XIV   A nineteenth-century enclosure road, Barrington, Cambridgeshire

XV   Ermine Street, Ancaster, Lincolnshire

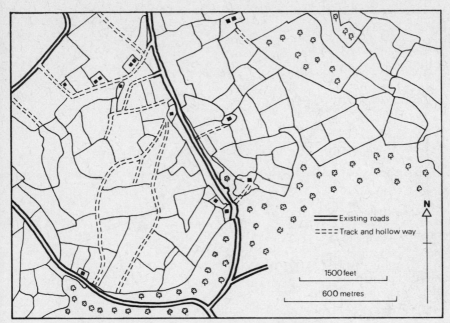

Fig. 74 Medieval forest tracks, Whiteparish, Wiltshire

passes through some of the 1330 fields, appears to have been in existence even earlier, perhaps by 968 at the latest. Similarly at Littleport, on the fens, one of the lanes there seems to be much earlier than the adjacent fields, and though in the final analysis we cannot ever date such tracks, there is every reason to suppose that they may be of Roman or even of prehistoric date.

The problem is even more complex on the open downlands, moorlands or mountainous areas of Britain for not only do we have tracks and holloways of every type there, but in these areas they were used for a variety of purposes until relatively recent times (Plates VII and VIII). We can point to the use in different ways and at different times of specific tracks, but we have no idea what date they are or when they were formed. Some, especially those in the Peak District and in Cornwall, we know were used by pack horses bringing down the products of early lead and tin mining. Others, on the Scottish borders and in the highlands, were used by raiding parties. Most were used for centuries, if not millennia, for local pack horse traffic between settlements.

Perhaps the most common use for many of these tracks, especially

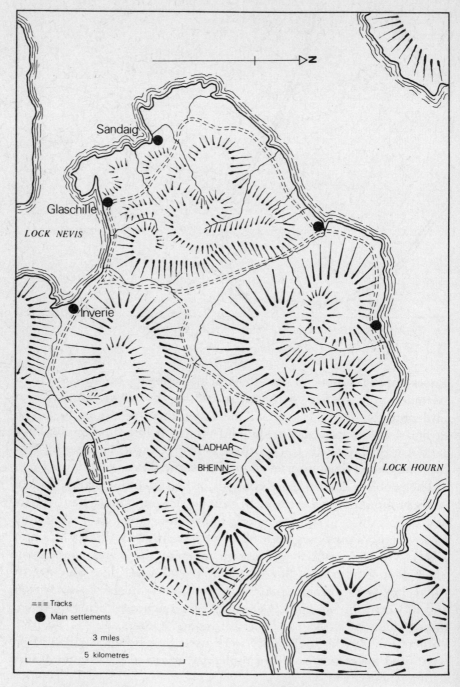

**Fig. 75 Transhumance tracks, Knoydart, Scotland**

in Wales, Scotland and northern England, was for the specific type
of pastoral farming there which is known as transhumance. This is
the system whereby herds and flocks are moved up from the lowlands where they are wintered to spend the summer months on the
highland or upland pastures. Transhumance, when fully developed,
was a complex organization which involved part of the human population moving with the animals and living on the mountains all
summer. So we find on the mountains today countless abandoned
and sometimes still occupied farmsteads, cottages and huts which
were used by the summer herdsmen. These are often known as shiel-
ings, and between them and leading down into the lowlands are
miles of tracks, along which the moving herds were driven. Sometimes the actual land used for the upland pasture was carefully
defined so that each lowland township or village had its own shieling
area, which could be up to seven miles from the townships to which
they belonged. The trackways along which the animals moved could,
therefore, produce an extensive and complex pattern.

One such area which has been studied in detail is that of
Knoydart, between Loch Nevis and Loch Hourn opposite the Isle of
Skye in western Scotland (Fig. 75). There, along the edges of the
lochs, is a series of small townships, made up of small scattered
farmsteads. Each township had an area of summer grazing upland in
the centre of the area up to six miles away. The township of Sandaig,
for instance, had its upland pasture three-and-a-half miles to the east
on the southern slopes of Ladhar Bheinn. The next township to the
south had its upland pasture four miles to the north-east on the
north-west side of Ladhar Bheinn. Thus the trackways from each
township to its pasture land, which indeed still exist, ran along the
coast and then turned north and north-east following the lower
ground. At the same time the trackways from another township
further east again, Inverie, ran north to meet the others and then on
to separate upland pastures two-and-a-half miles to the north. The
tracks from other townships around the coast met and crossed these
at various points, so creating the complex pattern that can still be
traced. Thus the purpose of these tracks is understood but we do not
know when they originated, or for how long they were in use. The
system of transhumance here lasted well into the nineteenth century,
which is how we know so much about it. It certainly existed in the
medieval period, and possibly for long before. We might even take
note of the existence of some Neolithic chambered tombs dating to

the third millenium BC which lie along the coast, very close to the existing townships, and presumably near to the as yet undiscovered prehistoric settlements which went with them. It is just possible, but certainly unprovable, that the builders of these tombs carried on a very similar way of life to the medieval farmers and that they too had a shieling economy. If so the origins of these medieval upland pastures, and thus the tracks which lead to them, may lie back in the prehistoric era.

After this long discussion of the various types and uses of medieval roads we must look briefly at their upkeep and repair. We can say at once that in most places this was negligible or nonexistent, and the rutted holloways and tracks which survive from this period show this well. Any movement along medieval roads was uncomfortable at best and unbelievably difficult at worst. Repair and upkeep of roads normally fell on the parish through which they passed, but the work was rarely carried out properly, if at all. Usually only the largest potholes were filled or complete blockages removed. Such repairs that were made were carried out as quickly and as cheaply as possible without any planning and the work was inevitably of a temporary nature. There are a number of good examples still surviving that show this haphazard method of repairing medieval roads, but perhaps the best is on the Dorset-Hampshire boundary alongside the Salisbury-Blandford Road. The section of this road on the Dorset side of the boundary follows the line of the old Roman road and thus must have been, at least in part, reasonably surfaced. But at the country boundary the medieval road swung north-east while the Roman road carried straight on. From this point the medieval road, running across chalk downland, must have degenerated into a rough track with innumerable wheel ruts and holes. These were no doubt periodically filled in by digging chalk from the adjacent land and dumping it into the worst of the ruts, a method which was typical of medieval road repairs, if not an entirely successful one. At the county boundary itself, however, the medieval road repairers must have realized that there was a source of material to fill the ruts close at hand, far better than the chalk normally used. This was the abandoned section of the Roman road which at this point had been surfaced with gravel. Thus the medieval people dug the gravel from the top of the Roman agger and carried it to the existing road a few yards away. However, as the two roads were diverging, it presumably became too much trouble to carry the gravel further and further to the medieval one and so the process was abandoned and the old method of using chalk continued. Today we can look at the Roman road and see that its great embankment or agger is neatly trenched all along its surface for a distance of about 200 yards from its junction with the medieval one; then the trench stops and the Roman road continues undamaged (Plate III).

The last feature of medieval roads to be examined, and one that perhaps survives best in the landscape, is that of bridges. In sharp contrast to the roads themselves, many medieval bridges, and particularly those of the fourteenth and fifteenth centuries, were remarkably well built and often of considerable architectural merit. In terms of structural engineering, many are incredibly strong. Until a recent bypass was built, the graceful bridge over the River Ouse between Godmanchester and Huntingdon, built about 1300 on the foundations of an older bridge to take the pack horse trains and lumbering carts of medieval times, took the full weight of traffic on a modern trunk road. Every day hundreds of vehicles, including scores of overweight continental container trucks, roared over it without any apparent structural damage. Medieval bridge builders built well.

Most medieval bridges were constructed and paid for by the benevolence of private individuals, corporate bodies who saw the commercial advantages or by charitable institutions. They were repaired by the owners of local estates, by the church or other organizations or by the receipts from tolls. All over Britain fine examples of medieval bridges funded by these means can still be seen. The bridge at Huntingdon, mentioned above, shows in its plan and design that it was built by two separate groups whose work joined in the centre. It is probable that each side was built by the authorities of the adjacent towns of Godmanchester on the south and Huntingdon on the north, both of whom had economic interests in keeping traffic moving. At nearby St Ives, as we saw earlier, the new town, founded by the Abbots of Ramsey about 1110, was joined to the old road system of the area by a new bridge, which was rebuilt in the late fourteenth or early fifteenth century and still remains today. Here again it was in the interests of the abbey to build their bridge and keep it in good repair in order to make sure that the town remained a commercial success. In this way the rents and tolls of the town continued to fill the ecclesiastical coffers.

While there are numerous fine medieval bridges of this kind all

over Britain, just as interesting and far more exciting to find are the
tiny medieval bridges hidden away on the byways of the land. Little
or nothing is known of the history of most of them, but they must
have been built at various times to serve local and long-distance
traffic by lords and ecclesiastics. One such is at the village of Char-
welton, in south-western Northamptonshire, where on the side of the
modern main road between Daventry and Banbury, and probably
quite unnoticed by most travellers, is a narrow bridge only about
fifteen yards long and two yards wide which carried the medieval
pack horse trains dryshod over the tiny River Cherwell. In the
north of the same county, at the village of Braybrooke and completely hidden from view by the modern road on top of it, is a small
thirteenth-century bridge (Plate IX). Here we have an example of a
changing route pattern, for though now the road over the bridge is a
minor one leading into the village, in medieval times it was the main
route north from St Albans via Bedford to Leicester. Today its
replacement, the A6, runs on the ridge top a mile to the north. But
this bridge indicates the earlier route in the valley bottom. On the
other hand, at Bishops Caundle, a tiny village deep in the Black-
moor Vale in north Dorset, there is a fifteenth-century bridge carrying a minor lane over the Caundle Brook. There is no indication that
this road was ever of great importance, and the bridge must have
been built merely to ease the passage of local traffic across the
marshy stream.

# 5 Post Medieval Roads and Tracks

The history of Dark Age and medieval roads and tracks was mainly one of unorganized development and change within an overall pattern laid down centuries before. In the period from the reign of Elizabeth I onwards, though slow change and evolution continued, and even increased, there was also a gradual development of the control and construction of roads, first by local authorities and other organizations and finally by the state itself. This situation is of course paralleled in many other aspects of life in the last 500 years, as society has become more complex, interdependent and mobile, but it is not necessarily as simple as it appears. It is easy to say, and indeed it has often been said, that the increasing mobility of population, growth of trade and industry, and improvements in vehicles all produced a demand for better roads which was satisfied only by increasing administrative control and developing new construction techniques. While this may be true to some extent, our experience of the history of twentieth-century roads should make us seek other explanations as well, for roads are not changed just by the demands of external pressures and events, they change their own environment and the social organization of their users. Once any improvement to a road is made, it starts to generate its own traffic. Thus while it may be that the demand for improved roads in order to move goods and people actually led to better roads, when these improvements were undertaken traffic volume and speed increased, leading to more demands, more improvements and more traffic. In the end the process becomes a vicious circle in which more and more government support and intervention is required and ultimately we reach the almost insoluble situation of the late twentieth century. This problem started to develop in the sixteenth century and though it gathered momentum very slowly at first, it is because of this situation that the story of post-medieval roads is, in part at least, different from that of the preceding one thousand years.

The first important move towards state control was the Highways Act of 1555, whereby the responsibility for maintaining roads in good condition was placed firmly upon the parishes through which they ran. It was not a success, however, because many parishes refused to carry out the work or could not possibly cope with the amount of repairs needed for, with the expanding economy of the time, traffic was also increasing substantially. In fact by the early seventeenth century it may safely be said that on the main routes of the country, as well as on many minor ones, there was more traffic than there had ever been. The country was changing with the impact of the Renaissance and the Reformation: new ideas, new techniques and new demands, as well as new interest in travel, all led to increased communication and thus more traffic. This change is reflected in the small-scale county and national maps which, for the first time, depicted roads. John Norden, for instance, marked roads on many of his maps, though in fact they are not to be trusted in detail; a number of other people also made surveys at this time.

The result of this increase in traffic and the failure of the attempts to improve roads meant that they still remained difficult to use. This was due in part to the failure to find a ubiquitous method of repair and maintenance, partly because the techniques of road construction were still very crude, and partly because of the increasing traffic. The latter is very important for from the mid sixteenth century onwards the development of regular carrier services between main towns occurred and considerable loads were being moved across the country. By 1600, for example, there was a thrice-weekly carrier between Ipswich and London and, in another sphere, coal from the Midlands Coalfield was being sent by pack horse trains in all directions for distances of forty miles or more. Also in the sixteenth century came the first real carriages which could give a reasonable degree of comfort for travellers with money. Up to that time everyone either rode on horses or was shaken to pieces in carts whose bodies were directly resting on the axles. Now carriages with the body slung on straps above the axles appeared and, though to our eyes they still look appallingly uncomfortable, they marked a great advance in contemporary passenger comfort.

When the 1555 Act was seen to have failed, various other statutes were enacted in the early seventeenth century, in an attempt to make the parish system of maintenance more effective. However, the lack of any central organization and control prevented real improvement. Then in 1663 a major step forward was achieved, when an Act of Parliament was passed which enabled the Justices of the Peace for Hertfordshire, Huntingdonshire and Cambridgeshire to levy tolls on travellers for the repair of that part of the Great North Road which passed through these counties. The first tollgate or turnpike was erected at Wadesmill in Hertfordshire, others followed along the same road, and a new era had dawned. This dawn was not an unblemished one, for the original Act was intended to remain in force for only eleven years, and though it was extended to twenty-one years in Hertfordshire, eventually it expired and the tollgates were removed. Nevertheless the advantages of this system were recognized and within a short time the Turnpike System, whereby those who used the roads were made to pay for them, became a well-established method of road maintenance and improvement. By 1700 seven Acts of Parliament authorizing Turnpike Trusts had been passed. From 1700 to 1750 they averaged ten a year and between 1750 and 1790 as many as forty a year. The last decade of the eighteenth century saw an average of fifty Acts of Parliament setting up Turnpike Trusts every year. Nor was this activity confined to England. The system was extended to Wales and parts of Scotland, also in the eighteenth century. One of the first turnpike roads in Wales was that from Shrewsbury to Wrexham in 1752, and by 1800 north Wales alone had 1000 miles of turnpike roads.

These turnpikes were usually controlled by locally elected trusts, small in scope and coping only with local needs, so they suffered from a lack of capital, central organization and any real control. Many were involved in little more than twenty or thirty miles of road at the most, and there was often little or no cooperation between adjacent trusts. Nor, in the eighteenth century at least, was there any real technical advance in the method of road construction or repair which enabled great improvements to be made to the road surfaces. Most repair work was carried out in the traditional way with potholes being filled with material from adjacent quarries, ruts being levelled and drainage ditches dug and recut. Yet turnpikes did have a considerable effect. Many local improvements were carried out. Excessive gradients were eased by deeper cuttings or embankments, sharp bends were removed and replaced by easier curves and often completely new diversions were made. Perhaps more important, in terms of the overall national road system, the turnpikes tended to reduce the multiplicity of older routes into a single line. The medieval situation, described in detail in the previous chapter, whereby a main route may have had two or three alternative ways across a specific area, was changed. Usually only one way was turn-piked and was thus used by most traffic. As a result, the lines of many of the trunk roads of today were finally established.

The best way of appreciating what effect the turnpikes had is to look at a specific example, such as the road between Cambridge and Newmarket, a distance of some fourteen miles (Fig. 76). The medieval road between the two towns was a very roundabout one. It left Cambridge running in an easterly direction, but just outside the village of Barnwell it swung north-east, parallel to the River Cam, a line now followed by the main road through a modern housing estate. When it reached the village of Fen Ditton it turned at right angles and ran for two miles south-east along the top of a Dark Age defensive dyke. It then crossed Quy Water, a small steam, at its narrowest point and turned north-east to run through the villages and across the common fields of Stow and Lode on an ancient fen-edge track. At Lode it turned south-east again and ran on to Bottisham village where, after passing along the main street, it started to climb the lower slopes of Newmarket Heath in an easterly direction. For the first mile-and-a-half the road ran through the common fields of Bottisham on a somewhat winding course. Then beyond the Bottisham fields the heath itself, a broad open area of grass-covered chalk downland, was reached. Here the road broke up into numerous tracks all heading generally north-east across the heath towards Newmarket. Another set of similar tracks joined the first from the south-east, these being in fact the main London to Norwich road at this point. A few miles short of Newmarket the heath is crossed by the great Dark Age ditch called the Devil's Dyke. When this was first built, perhaps in the fifth or sixth century AD, it completely blocked all routes across the heath. In medieval times, however, a large number of gaps were cut through it, and it was via these that the numerous tracks from Cambridge and London passed and then ran together to enter the main street of Newmarket.

In 1745 the section of this road from Cambridge to Bottisham was taken over by the then newly formed Godmanchester to Newmarket Heath Turnpike Trust. The first two miles of the road out of Cambridge were merely improved, but beyond Barnwell a new two-and-a-quarter mile section was cut running along broad curves to

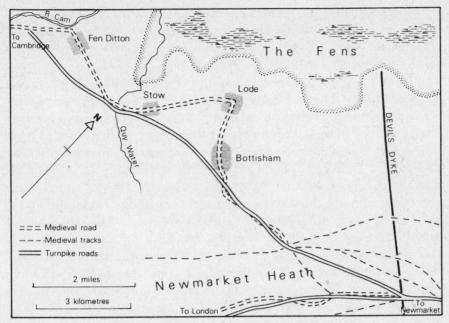

Fig. 76 Medieval and turnpike roads, Cambridge-Newmarket

the Quy Water crossing. This was not a completely new road, for the
Turnpike Commissioners merely widened and built up two old lanes
through the common fields of Teversham and Fen Ditton. From Quy
Bridge to Bottisham, however, a completely new road was built, well
to the south of Stow and Lode, not only shortening the distance by
one-and-a-half miles, but cutting out the succession of sharp bends
at Stow and the right-angled corner at Lode. This new road was on
a broad curve and it actually cut right across a number of the strips
in the common fields of Stow. At the southern end of Bottisham the
new road rejoined the old road and the latter, widened and somewhat straightened, became the turnpike road as it passed through
the strips of Bottisham fields. The point at which the common fields
ended and the heath began is clearly marked today for from then on
the present road runs straight for exactly half a mile until, at the
highest point of the heath, on the Turnpike Trust's boundary, the
improved road finished abruptly and traffic returned to the older
tracks. This situation lasted for some years until 1763 when another
Turnpike Trust, that for Newmarket Heath, was set up. At first the
Trust was only concerned with the London to Newmarket road and

it changed this from a multitude of tracks to a broad way 100 feet wide, cut in long straight alignments across the heath and passing through the Devil's Dyke via one of the largest medieval gaps. Here, at an ideal place, a tollgate was erected. Then in 1775 the Trust took control of the route from the end of the Godmanchester Trust's road to Newmarket. The old tracks were again replaced by an exactly straight two-and-a-half mile road, also 100 feet wide, laid out across the heath to join the London road at the tollgate at the Devil's Dyke. The whole length of this section of the road was then marked by neat milestones. However, though these roads were easily established all was not to be well with the Newmarket Heath's Trust. While honest travellers followed the new London and Cambridge roads, duly paid their tolls at the turnpike gate and passed on, a large number of people avoided the tollgate completely. This was because, though the new roads had been laid across the heath, the heath itself remained open downland. As travellers approach the tollgate, they merely swung off the road, moved across the heath and passed through the Devil's Dyke via the old medieval gaps, then rejoined the new road beyond the tollgate and continued their journey without payment. This situation did not suit the Turnpike Trust for obvious reasons, so they ordered that the medieval gaps in the dyke should be blocked up by the construction of banks across them. Accordingly, this was done, but at once there was an outcry from the most powerful organization in the area, the Jockey Club at Newmarket. At that time, as today, there were two racecourses on Newmarket Heath, one on either side of the Devil's Dyke. The Jockey Club complained that by blocking the gaps, people attending race meetings could not get to the courses, so a compromise was reached whereby the Turnpike Trust put small gaps in their blocking banks and built gates in them which were kept locked except on race days. The Jockey Club was satisfied, the Turnpike Trust received its dues and the Cambridge to Newmarket road was fixed on the alignment followed by the A45 until the construction of the present Newmarket bypass.

Apart from the curious and unusual dispute with the Jockey Club, this lengthy description of the history of this road typifies much of that of the turnpike era with its mixture of new cuts and improvements to old roads and the erection of tollgates and milestones. The two latter features are, of course, those which still mark many of these old turnpikes today, for though the gates themselves have long since gone, the small round or polygonal dwellings built for the gate-keepers, often with projecting bays so that they could see approaching traffic, are a common feature. The variety of stone and the later cast-iron milestones which belong to this era also still survive in many places.

Turnpike roads, as all roads, also affected the landscape through which they passed. Just as the changes in medieval roads altered medieval villages and towns, so the turnpike changed them too. Sometimes it was the architecture of places which was altered. This is especially true of the late eighteenth and early nineteenth centuries when the great coaching age reached its peak. All towns and even small villages which lay on the route of regular and frequent coach traffic soon took on a new appearance. Numerous inns, usually in brick or fine stone, with broad carriage archways leading into a stable yard, were improved or built anew at this time (Plate X). Marlborough in Wiltshire, on the London to Bath road, is typical of this type of town, and villages on main routes often have one or two fine eighteenth-century inns.

In other places the turnpikes actually altered the shapes of villages. In the village where this book is being written, Whittlesford in Cambridgeshire, one can see this well. The main medieval village street lay on a very old east to west road and crossing it, near its centre, was a less important north to south road. In the early eighteenth century this minor road was made a turnpike for traffic to and from Cambridge. As a result the old main street lost its importance and when ribbon development started in the nineteenth century it took place along the new improved road, not along the old one. Thus the village changed from a linear one along a single street to one arranged around a cross-roads.

Occasionally turnpike roads actually created new places. On the Wiltshire-Hampshire border where the old medieval road between Salisbury and Romsey passed through the parish of Sherfield English and the eastern part of the parish of Whiteparish, it followed a winding route, deeply hollowed between steep, narrow banks which can still be seen today (Fig. 77). In 1756 the whole road was turnpiked and though, over most of its length, the old road was merely widened and straightened, the section in Whiteparish and Sherfield was diverted along an almost straight line two-and-a-half miles long, well to the south of the older one. Near the point where the new part joined the old road, the Whiteparish tollgate was set up and over the next fifty years a small group of cottages was built there producing a new hamlet with the name of Cowsfield Gate. To the east, in Sherfield, another new hamlet grew up on the turnpike road. This was so successful that when the parish church was rebuilt in the nineteenth century it was erected in the new hamlet and not in the original village of Sherfield.

The establishment of thousands of miles of turnpike roads led to a huge increase in traffic which eventually threatened the very system itself. In the 1720s, when turnpikes were new, Daniel Defoe could wax eloquent about them. He said that they were 'very great things' and that they were 'easy to travellers and to carriages as well as to cattle'. But as the century advanced and traffic multiplied, complaints about the state of turnpikes increased. Arthur Young, travelling in the 1760s and 70s, described some turnpikes as terrible, infamous or execrable. Part of the trouble was that the turnpike system itself was inefficient, but by far the most important reason was the increase in traffic that the roads themselves had generated – for the effect on trade, as Defoe said, was 'incredible'. Many roads were 'exceedingly throng'd' with 'a vast number of carriages' carrying agricultural produce, with 'infinite droves of black cattle, hogs and sheep' as well as pack horses, mail and ordinary travellers on horseback.

The eighteenth century was also the great era of coaching. The improved roads and better coach design increased the speed of travel considerably: the journey from London to York still took four days in 1754, but by 1774 it was reduced to two. In 1784 the government started to send the Royal Mail by coach, at first between London and Bristol, and the result was a huge incentive for speed which was in turn reflected in passenger travel.

There were continuous attempts by the State to improve roads in the eighteenth century: various acts of parliament tried to enforce the use of broad wheels, for example, to prevent the formation of deep ruts, but all without success. By the end of the century, some advances were being made in the techniques of road construction, though the implementation of these ideas was slow to catch on. John Metcalf (1717–1810) was one of the first engineers to advocate solid foundations and good drainage, and further developments were carried out by J. L. Macadam (1756–1836), whose name has become part of our language. Macadam encouraged the laying of solid foundations of broken stone which were then watered and rolled to form

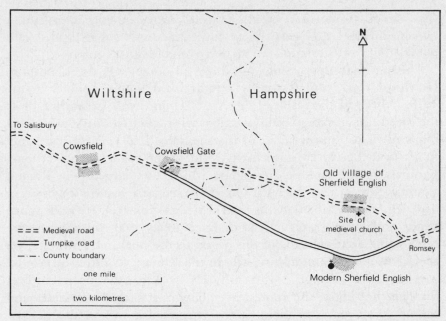

Fig. 77 Medieval and turnpike roads, Whiteparish, Wiltshire and Sherfield
English, Hampshire

a hard, smooth surface. At the same time, in the new industrial
areas, surplus slag and cinder were often used to repair and build
roads. Industry, too, provided other materials in the form of iron for
bridges, though most of the numerous bridges that were built in the
eighteenth century were still of stone. It was not until the nineteenth
century that the use of iron for bridges became common.

By 1821 over 18,000 miles of English roads had been turnpiked,
with another 2000 miles in Wales. The products of agriculture,
commerce and industry flowed along them in vast quantities as well
as mail and an increasing number of travellers. Yet the system was
still a poor one. Quite apart from the inadequacies of the turnpikes
themselves there were huge gaps in the system: by 1837 only 18 per
cent of all the highways in east Yorkshire were turnpiked and in
East Anglia, Cornwall, and Devon it was as low as 10 per cent. In
Wales the figures were even smaller. Most British roads remained in
their medieval form but, as a result of increased traffic, in a far worse
state. The great turnpiked highways are the ones that catch the
imagination in this period, but we must not forget that they were a

very small proportion of the whole. Government intervention remained either non existent or futile and only when there were political or strategic implications were any advances made.

The one road that stands out above all others was the London to Holyhead road, almost totally rebuilt by Thomas Telford in the 1820s. This was the result of the Act of Union with Ireland in 1801: the need for rapid communication with that country was now imperative, so improvement of the main road to Ireland was sanctioned and the work commenced. Most of the road was an old one, particularly the south-eastern part which was largely the Roman Watling Street, now the A5. On these sections narrow parts were widened, new embankments and culverts constructed and sharp bends and steep gradients eased. Even today one can still see the remarkable achievements of this work: to the north of Towcester on the A5 in Northamptonshire, where the Roman Watling Street ran over a series of high ridges athwart its line, the deep cuttings through the ridges, the approach embankments up the hillsides and the sweeping curves to avoid narrow, steep-sided valleys all still exist despite many later alterations. In some places, however, the Holyhead Road was made anew, and this is nowhere better seen than on Anglesey itself. In medieval times there was no main route across the island, but in 1765 a turnpike had been authorized to run from the Menai Straits to Holyhead. The turnpike merely improved one of the existing roads via Penmynydd, Llangefni and Llanynghenedl. Telford's new road completely ignored this route and was cut straight across Anglesey from his new suspension bridge to Holyhead in a series of straight alignments.

Road improvement work such as Telford's Holyhead Road and a number of others of the same date, including some of the trans-Pennine routes, may have been viewed at the time as the beginning of a new era. If it was so considered, however, it was a mistake, for other events and developments were taking place which were to stifle the potential of early nineteenth-century road improvement. The appearance of canals in the late eighteenth century, which took much long-distance bulk traffic and even passengers away from the roads, was already a prelude to this, but it was the railway that dealt the death blow to the turnpikes and the other major routes. The rapid development of the British railway system resulted not only in the abandonment of many long-distance roads for goods traffic, but for passenger traffic as well. The long-distance carriers and the famous stage coaches all disappeared and the revenues of the Turnpike Trusts plummeted. From 1860 dis-turnpiking was actively pursued; only 184 trusts remained in 1881 and the last vanished in 1895. The trunk roads of Britain had to wait for the internal combustion engine to give them a new lease of life.

The turnpikes, although major roads, were by no means the only important long-distance roads of the eighteenth and nineteenth centuries. In many parts of Britain there was an equally important set of routes of older origin which were just as widely used at this time, the drove roads and pack horse tracks. These types of road covered the entire British Isles, though where they are best preserved today, as abandoned holloways and tracks, they are in the upland areas. This accident of survival, or rather the lack of later alteration, should not allow us to fall into the trap of thinking that drove roads or pack horse trails existed only there: they were everywhere and lived on side by side with the turnpikes until well into the nineteenth century.

To illustrate this we may take the example of the Great North Road in Huntingdonshire, already examined in detail in the previous chapter. We saw how, in medieval times, there were at least three alternative routes across the county, practically all in use at the same time. With the turnpike road improvements of the eighteenth century the main route for wheeled traffic became fixed on the most easterly of these three alignments and so the present A1 came into being. But the alternative routes still remained in use, not by wheeled vehicles, but by vast herds of animals which were moved constantly from the north of England and Scotland to the urban centres of the south.

Such drove roads were once common all over Britain but, like almost all the roads discussed in this book, they are virtually impossible to date. They could, indeed, have been described in any of the previous chapters and the only reason for including them here is that it was at this period that they reached their peak in terms of the traffic they carried. It is not easy to recognize these drove roads for a number of reasons. One is the usual, that most are still with us, and that hedged and tarmaced they look the same as other roads of very different origins. Another is that, even where they survive and can be recognized in the upland areas of Britain, they are indistinguishable from transhumance routes (indeed the functions were interchangeable). Some drove roads were for local and relatively short-

distance movement of animals, others were for droving cattle over
hundreds of miles. In addition local and long-distance pack horse
trails were also inextricably mixed up with the droveways and, as
always, we have very little clear documentation which indicates the
period of use or function.

A brief look at the various types of these roads is the best way of
approaching the complexities of the situation and appreciating the
regional differences. In north Wales, for example, many drove roads
and pack horse trails have been identified, running along the main
valleys and crossing the mountain passes. They are generally recognizable as sinuous hollows three to six feet wide at the bottom and of
varying depth. They usually follow a course, dictated purely by the
nature of the country traversed, and are frequently divided into a
number of parallel routes. Such a description is equally suitable for
prehistoric, Roman or medieval trackways, and thus the dating of
them becomes impossible. Indeed such roads are probably of all these
periods. In north Wales, there are additional features which are of
interest: for example, though they are impassable for wheeled vehicles, in some places long stretches are deliberately paved, especially
where they cross marshy areas and even rough causeways have been
constructed. On steep ground they are sometimes either cut into
deliberate zig-zags or built up into steps. A particularly good example of the latter is at Bont Pen-y-benglog at the west end of Llyn
Ogwen in Caernarvonshire, where the route climbs up the moun-
tainside in a series of crude steps. This particular place was
described in 1773 as 'the most dreadful horse path in Wales'. These
instances of apparent deliberate construction hint at some form of
local authority, for it is unlikely that the drovers or pack horse driv-
ers or individual local inhabitants would have involved themselves in
work of this kind. Yet no record of such authorities exists.

Another excellent example of a worn and rutted pack horse road
in the same area is in the valley just west of Capel Curig. Though
the modern road leading to the Llanberis Pass is actually on the line
of the earlier track along most of the valley, at its east end above
Llynnau Mymbyr the original trail lies north of the present road and
is preserved largely intact.

Many of these drove roads were probably for local traffic, but
others formed part of a much more complex system whereby Welsh
cattle were driven to English markets. Even in the thirteenth century, recorded by the first surviving documents, there was a well-

established droving trade from all parts of Wales to markets at
Gloucester and Shrewsbury, and even further into England. These
drove roads remained important until the coming of the railways,
and especially in the eighteenth and early nineteenth centuries were
crowded with herds and flocks being driven to the expanding urban
areas of England. In the uplands of Wales there were hundreds of
miles of minor local routes, such as those described above, along
which the animals were moved. Gradually these coalesced into main
routes which crossed the border into England. One of the best
known of these was the one from Montgomery to Shrewsbury.
Montgomery, high on the edge of the Welsh uplands, was the focus
of innumerable routes from the surrounding mountains. From there,
thousands of animals were moved south-east along what is the modern road to Bishop's Castle where other herds from the adjacent
mountains joined them. Then the herds moved on east via a variety
of routes, all of which are either main roads or narrow country lanes
today, to Plowden at the southern tip of The Long Mynd (Fig. 78).
Here, to take advantage of open pastures, they climbed the steep

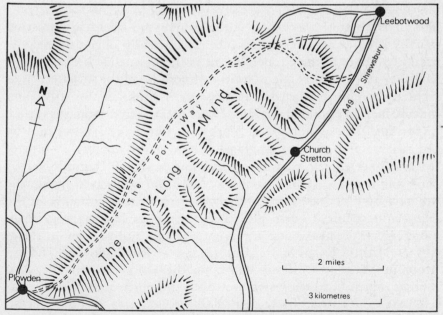

Fig. 78 Drove roads, The Long Mynd, Shropshire

slopes to Black Knoll and followed The Port Way, an alleged prehistoric track, along the crest of The Long Mynd. At its northern end the drovers moved their cattle off the mountain, through various old lanes north of Church Stretton and on to the present Shrewsbury to Ludlow road at Leebotwood. From there they moved north to Shrewsbury along what is now the main A49 trunk road.

Another quite different area, where drove roads and pack horse ways are still clearly visible in the landscape, though equally difficult to date, is the moorland of the southern Pennines. Here again the observant can detect an extensive web of narrow trackways and hollows all over the moors, clearly the product of centuries of use. They range from local paths leading from villages to long-distance routes linking the towns beyond the moors. As in Wales and elsewhere these are marked by holloways or trenches, often duplicated so that broad areas of the hillsides are cut into deep furrows.

One of the best places to see good droveways and pack horse trails is on the moors south-west of Sheffield, on either side of the Derwent Valley. The old track on the moors across Bradwell Edge, leading down into Bradwell, a village south-east of Castleton in Derbyshire, for example, is cut ten feet into the hillside as it descends in a series of zig-zags. There is also evidence on these moors of sections of paved pack horse ways: there are several on Big Moor, east of Froggatt, also in Derbyshire, occurring either where the tracks are crossing marshy ground or where the route was already obviously heavily used. The date of their construction is unknown but it is probable that they are relatively late in time and perhaps of the seventeenth or eighteenth century when traffic was at its peak. In this area, and indeed in other upland regions, where extractive industries were important, such as north-west Yorkshire, the Lake District and on the moors of south-west England, there is yet another system of tracks connected with various local mining activities. In north Derbyshire and south Yorkshire, coal was dug from crude bell-pits on the uplands from at least the seventeenth century and certainly in the eighteenth century. These pits, and the tracks leading from them along which the pack horse trains moved, can still be seen on Eyam Moor, north of Eyam in Derbyshire and at Ringinglow on Hallam Moor in Yorkshire. Further south on the limestone uplands, lead mining, much of which lasted well into the nineteenth century, has left other trackways. There, especially in the area of Peak Forest, Castleton and Tideswell, we can still see very broad green lanes, often running at right angles off the main through roads. These appear to have no purpose, but they all run up to abandoned lead mines. They were the result of the eighteenth- and nineteenth-century miners setting out very broad access roads to their workings, though it is clear that only pack horses were ever used along them. These relatively late tracks, connected with industry, are common and only serve to confuse the pattern of earlier drove and pack horse trails, especially where they are identical in form.

By far the best and most impressive of the still visible drove roads lie in the north, in Scotland and on the borders. All over Scotland the mountains are crossed by abandoned or little used tracks, which follow the valley bottoms and then climb steeply over narrow passes. In a sense they are ageless, in origin probably prehistoric; they have been used by raiders and cattle thieves for centuries, and when at last they are recorded in documents, usually not before the seventeenth or eighteenth century, they are often well-trodden drove roads. There are endless examples which any keen explorer will find. One such is a winding track which leaves the busy road between Aviemore and the ski slopes of the Cairngorms and runs south through the lower forests, around Loch An Eilein and on up the now largely empty Glen Feshie. Nothing is known of its history except as a nineteenth-century cattle drove road but its name Rathad Nam Mearlach, 'the thieves' road', indicates older and more unlawful uses.

Elsewhere in Scotland, as well as in the north of England, one can still trace some of the great drove roads which often run for miles across the uplands leading south to the English markets. As with the Welsh examples, cattle tended to be brought along the local drove-ways to main collection centres where they were then taken on by professional drovers to the major towns of the lowlands or across the border to England. The droving of cattle from the highlands of Scotland to England is first recorded as an already important large-scale business in the early seventeenth century and it must have had much older origins. In attained its greatest proportions about 1827 after which it declined and was finally killed by the railways. One of the main collecting centres or 'trysts' was Falkirk in Stirlingshire near the head of the Firth of Forth. From there the drovers moved southeast along what are now main roads via Bathgate and Mid Calder and then climbed up the steep north-west face of the Pentland Hills and down the Lyne Water Valley to Cauldstane and Romannobridge. From here they followed what is now the A72 road to Peebles and then climbed over the uplands across the south-west part of Roxburghshire to Newcastleton and thence over the border into the North Tyne Valley.

Parts of this route have been examined in some detail by experienced scholars and the results, far too long to describe in detail here, are remarkable. They show better than anywhere else the complexity of drove roads, especially in mountainous areas. All the features already noted as occurring elsewhere are visible, though here over many miles of country. Parts of the drove roads are farm tracks, country lanes and even main roads. Elsewhere multiple tracks, terraces and gigantic holloways all occur. Sometimes, as at Muslee, south-west of Hawick, the later fields have been laid out to leave a wide green lane flanked by dry-stone walls to allow the passage of large numbers of beasts. There is also some evidence of deliberate construction of the track in places, as on the Selkirk-Roxburgh border near Kingside Loch where a thirty-foot wide stone culvert, far too broad for foot or pack horse traffic, carries the drove road over a small burn. There are also many points where the way divides into a number of alternate tracks, often two or three miles apart, which then converge again. In addition, all along the route, other local droveways join the main one.

Inextricably mixed with all these are other tracks used for moving animals to the upland summer pastures from the valleys below. It is almost impossible to work out the full complexity of the drove system, particularly as most of the details of its working were never written down. In any case the real answer, as always, is that to define these ways as merely drove roads is to beg the question. If we look carefully at them we soon become aware that in many cases the drovers were almost the last people to use them. In Northumberland, for example, there are many long sections of holloways and tracks on the Simonside Hills which were certainly used by eighteenth-century drovers. But these tracks are also closely associated with prehistoric settlements, Roman forts and medieval villages. Some are known to have been used by invading Scottish armies in the Middle Ages, by cattle raiders across the border in the same period, by pedlars in the seventeenth century, by smugglers of illicit whisky in the eighteenth century, as well as by drovers; names such as Salters Road, Colway and Thieves' Track also indicate the former uses of these routes. Again we are looking at an ageless system of

communications which has continuously changed its form and layout over millenia and which is still partly used today, whether as a
main trunk road, a country lane or a hikers' path.

In the eighteenth century the uplands of Scotland also saw the
first real major road construction schemes in Britain since the
Roman period and which were, like them, based on military considerations. These roads resulted from the highland uprisings of 1715
and 1745 and, in particular, after 1724 when General Wade was sent
to the highlands to examine the situation there. He reported that
there were no real roads and that until there were, no firm control
could be maintained over the area. As a result a large programme of
road building was undertaken by the army, a process which produced the well-known Military Roads of Scotland (Fig. 79;
Plate IX). They have often been compared with the Roman roads of
northern England and southern Scotland because of their methods of
construction and their strategic basis. In fact this is not an exact
parallel, for the highland roads of the eighteenth century compare
very badly with the Roman roads in almost every aspect; some of

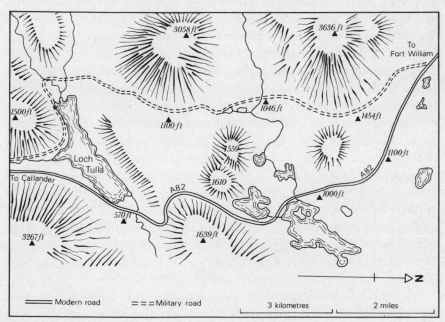

Fig. 79 Military road, Glenorchy, Argyll, Scotland

these are worth looking at in detail to see the alleged comparisons in a true light. Certainly the highland roads were similar to the Roman roads in terms of deliberate construction and some overall building details. They were planned to a standard width of six feet, and they were meant to have good foundations and well-built surfaces, with ditches, culverts, bridges and drains where necessary. They were constructed entirely by army personnel and linked various forts and garrisons dotted about the highlands, but they also differed from Roman roads in a number of ways, particularly in that they were built over a much longer period than the Roman roads. In contrast to the Romans' achievement of constructing the main military road system of northern England in two years the British army in Scotland took over seventy years. The Perth-Inverness road, for example, took eight years to build, between 1725 and 1733, with 300 men employed on various sections, while it took three years to build the road between Fort Augustus and Inverness.

Other differences between these roads and the Roman ones can best be seen by looking at one of them in detail, such as part of the Perth to Fort George Road between Braemar and Spittal of Glenshee. This section, although less than twenty miles in length, took well over a year to build. It followed the line of a much older route, and indeed the main A93 road has followed much of it today: where the modern road has not obliterated the original work, many constructional details can be seen. Usually it is a low causeway of boulders, with stone edges or kerbs, twelve to eighteen feet wide. On steep slopes it survives as a terrace thirteen to seventeen feet across with a kerb of boulders on the downhill side. Sometimes there are side ditches, and sometimes run-off drains downslope. Though most small streams seem to have been crossed by fords, a number of well-built culverts exist, and on larger streams good bridges were erected. At Fraser's Bridge, the original bridge of two rounded arches and a central pier, though much altered, still stands. Where it crosses damp or marshy ground stone causeways exist, and elsewhere the road makers seem to have tried to take advantage of areas which were relatively dry, such as glacial ridges and hummocks. Here wide cuttings were dug. Quarry pits, from which material was obtained, are also common features along the road.

All this sounds impressive, and comparable with the Roman roads, but if these constructional details are looked at very carefully indeed they tell us a good deal about the troops who built these

roads, and it is not always greatly to their credit. The overall alignments, for example, show very little sign of being reconnoitered or
planned as a whole, a feature which is always obvious in Roman
roads. The engineers were evidently content to remain in or near the
lowest parts of valleys until forced to extricate themselves at the cost
of excessive gradients or almost impossible zig-zag courses. Considerable lack of competence is also visible in such matters as drainage
and surfacing. Large sections were often overdeepened to form flat-
bottomed ditches which held water, and drains were often wrongly
levelled or badly cut. In other places no real foundations or proper
surfacing were provided and soft rock which soon disintegrated
seems to have been used.

On the whole the eighteenth-century military roads of Scotland
compare badly with Roman ones in the same area. Nevertheless,
they can be counted as a success in that they not only carried out
their original function but in many cases were the basis of later
routes, which we still use today whether as main trunk roads, minor
byways or for such widely ranging purposes as forestry, access to
National Grid pylon lines and agriculture.

The basic framework of these military roads was later filled in by
other roads both in Scotland and across the border. These, though
often planned for strategic purposes, were built either entirely by
civilians or pushed through by commercial pressures on the government. The road from the English border near Gretna, west to Port
Patrick, for example, was built for military use in 1763. This was
not new, and existing tracks seem to have been merely improved by
resurfacing and the addition of drainage ditches and new bridges.
Yet it was in a sense more a commercial road than a strategic one
and was regarded as such from its outset. An even better instance is
the military road from Newcastle to Carlisle, first planned after
appalling difficulties in moving troops across the area during the
1745 uprising. Its final authorization, however, was as much a result
of pressure from local landowners and tradesmen as from the army.
It was constructed entirely by civilian labour and was eventually
operated as a turnpike with tollgates.

All the various types of roads used or constructed in the post-
medieval period were important for the developing economy of
Britain in these centuries, but by far the most important roads, and
certainly the ones that remain most obviously in the landscape
today, are those that resulted from the enclosure movement of the

eighteenth and early nineteenth centuries. This movement was not, of course, directly concerned with roads. It was largely the result of agricultural changes whose origins and development are beyond the scope of this book. What in fact happened, in simple terms, was the physical dividing up into enclosed fields of tens of thousands of acres of agricultural land which up to the eighteenth century, was either common or open arable fields, undrained fen or moorland wastes. This process was carried out parish by parish or township by township, usually, but not always, following formal acts of parliament. In effect all the open land in each area, whether arable or pasture, was divided into enclosed fields, allotted to landowners in proportion to their former land holdings and various rights of common.

In the course of carrying out this work it was impossible to allot compact blocks of land without altering, to a greater or lesser extent, the existing road systems. In the areas of common arable the multitude of access ways and tracks passing along and around the blocks of strips were impossible to incorporate within the new enclosed field systems and on downlands and moorlands, the various trackways were a similar problem. As a result, in most places where enclosure took place in the eighteenth or nineteenth centuries, the existing road pattern was swept away and a new and simpler one laid down. As the actual work of dividing up the land was carried out by professional surveyors, and as surveyors always find it easier to work in straight lines, not only did the new fields tend to have straight sides but the new roads between them were also laid out, as far as possible, in straight alignments. The outcome was what seems to be a completely new road system over large parts of Britain.

The process was not ubiquitous. In many places it did not occur, for where the common fields had been enclosed, or the forests and wastes cleared and divided up into fields centuries before, there was no need for change. But over large parts of the Midlands, southern and north-eastern England and on the lower mountain slopes of northern England, Wales and Scotland the new fields and the new road systems appeared together. In these areas the greater part of the minor communication pattern of the present day is the result of the enclosure movement. On the whole the main roads, or at least what were main through roads at that time, were left largely unaltered except for minor widening or straightening, but most of the lesser roads were made anew. They are often clearly recognizable today as being exactly straight, with usually a standard width

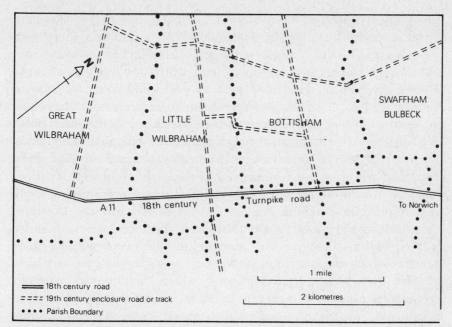

Fig. 80 Enclosure and turnpike roads and tracks, Wilbraham, Bottisham and Swaffham, Cambridgeshire

between the boundary hedges or walls of thirty, forty or occasionally sixty feet (Plates XII, XIII and XIV). Where they change alignment they do so either on the tops of hills, rather like the earlier Roman roads, or, and more especially, on parish boundaries (Fig. 80). The reason for the former is that the eighteenth- and nineteenth-century surveyors, like the Roman road engineers, used the hill tops as sighting points. The changes of alignment on parish boundaries almost always occur because the date of enclosure in one parish was rarely the same as that of the adjacent ones: the enclosure surveyor in parish *A* would lay out a new straight road from the village to the point on the boundary where the old road to the village in parish *B* was located; later the surveyor of parish *B* would lay out the new road from that village to the end of the new road in parish *A*. Thus over a wide area of Britain a pattern of straight roads with sharp changes of alignment developed which is still very obvious today.

As usual, however, it is easiest to look in some detail at a single example to show exactly what happened. This can be done

splendidly at Whittlesford, in south Cambridgeshire (Fig. 81), where
the enclosure of the parish took place in 1812. At that time there were
two main roads, three minor roads and numerous access ways into
and through the common or open fields which occupied most of the
land of the parish. The main east to west road from Royston to
Newmarket ran along the southern boundary. It was not altered by
enclosure and does not concern us here. Neither was the main north
to south road which passed through the village changed. Though an
old road of minor importance in medieval times, it had been
turnpiked and thus much improved in the early eighteenth century.
In addition to these there were three lesser roads, one running south
to the village of Duxford, one north-west to Newton and the third
westwards to Thriplow. Finally there were the access ways which led
only to various parts of the open fields and meadows. All these
minor roads and access ways were swept away in 1812 and replaced
by just four new public highways whose layout was carefully
arranged to achieve two objectives: to reconnect the village with its
neighbours, and to allow as easy an access as possible to the new
fields.

The work was made somewhat easier by the fact that all the surrounding parishes were still unenclosed at that time, and so the
Whittlesford surveyor could place his new roads where it was most
convenient. One of these was laid out exactly straight north-west
from the village to the point where the older track through the open
fields of Newton crossed the parish boundary. This new road was
not only a necessary through route but it also gave easy access to the
lord of the manor's new fields, which lay to the west of it, and to the
ten small fields of minor village farmers to the east. From this road a
short length of track was laid out west to the top of a chalk-capped
hill in order to allow villagers access to the parish chalk pit which
was then opened for them. (The pit was important for it provided
the blocks of hard chalk which was the main building material for
houses at that time.) The third road, also a major one, was laid out
straight from the west end of the village in a southerly direction to
join the main through road along the southern boundary of the parish. It also met the end of a track through the common fields of
Duxford parish in the south and in addition, it provided easy access
to the new fields of the second major landowner, as well as to those
of the vicar, Pembroke College Cambridge and five other small
landowners. These three new roads, as well as the main east to west

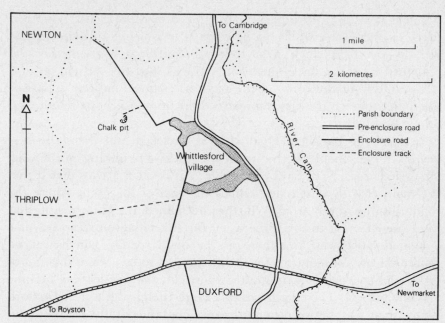

Fig. 81 Enclosure roads, Whittlesford, Cambridgeshire

and north to south existing roads, provided internal and external communication for the whole of the parish with one exception, in the south-west. Before enclosure there was a track leading west from the village across this area to the next village, Thriplow. It was not an important route in the early nineteenth century, though clearly it had been in the medieval period, for both Thriplow and Whittlesford villages grew up along this east to west routeway. By 1812, for reasons which are unknown, there was not much traffic between the two villages and the old road was abandoned. However, in order to gain access to the new fields in this corner of the parish, which included those belonging to the village charity, some belonging to the lord of the manor and a few owned by twelve small farmers, the last of the new roads was laid out to run across this area a little to the south of the old road. The new road stopped 200 yards short of the parish boundary but the enclosure authorities did lay out a footpath to carry it through to an old path in the Thriplow fields.

Thus the enclosure road system of Whittlesford was established, but for all its new development it still retained much of the older pattern. The main through roads, one of which was the prehistoric

Icknield Way, and the other, the turnpiked medieval road, remained much as they were, while the new roads to Newton and Duxford as well as the field track west towards Thirplow were merely the realigned routes of three much older tracks. But this system, even if it was only a modification of the past, was almost entirely a parish-orientated one. Later developments were to cause both major and minor problems.

In 1822 the parish of Duxford was enclosed and there the surveyor's replacement for the medieval trackway running north was, for various reasons of land ownership, cut in such a way that it met the main east to west road well to the east of the point where the road running south from Whittlesford joined it. This meant that local travellers on this road between the two villages had to traverse a long dog-leg onto and then off the main road – which was no doubt of little consequence for the 1820s, but today, when this minor cross-country road is a commuter short cut, the dog-leg has become a traffic hazard. The employees of a large chemical plant at Duxford dodge their way between long-distance container traffic on the main road at 8.45 every morning.

In 1845 the common fields of Thriplow to the west were enclosed. The enclosure of Whittlesford had already caused a change of routes here in that the Thriplow track eastwards to Whittlesford could not be used as its continuation in the latter parish had been abandoned already. In 1845, therefore, the original medieval track of Thriplow was replaced by a new one in order to join the end of the Whittlesford footpath. But to do this it had to leave Thriplow village in a very awkward place and when it reaches the Whittlesford boundary its junction is marked by a characteristic minor change of alignment. In addition, as the Whittlesford route was only a footpath at its western end, no wheeled traffic could pass between the two villages. Again this probably did not matter in the mid nineteenth century, but today the shortest way from Whittlesford to Thriplow by car involves a journey of over four miles instead of the two along the medieval track and the enclosure footpath. This also has interesting social implications, for there is far less contact between the villages of Whittlesford and Thriplow than there is between Whittlesford and Duxford. A surveyor's decision in the mid nineteenth century can, therefore, have wide-ranging results today.

As with all routes, enclosure roads also changed the physical appearance of towns and villages to a great extent. At a simple level the post-enclosure growth of villages has often been affected by the pattern of enclosure roads laid out for purely agricultural purposes. Far more important, however, is the effect on the growth of towns in the later nineteenth century. One good example is the city of Cambridge, where the expansion of the town across its former open fields was a complex process involving land ownership, new field shapes and cheap land. But the great south-western growth of Cambridge between 1820 and 1900 was basically along the road laid out by the enclosure surveyors as a minor track. Without this track, other things being equal, modern Cambridge would have taken on a very different shape. The same applies to many other of our major urban areas.

By the middle of the nineteenth century our present road system was virtually complete. It had evolved slowly over thousands of years from natural animal tracks through prehistoric ways, Roman roads, Saxon lanes, medieval highways, droveways, turnpikes and enclosure roads. It had been adapted slowly over the centuries to take account of changes both long term and short term. It had many faults, mostly the result of its long history. The twentieth century was, through its advanced technology, to bring those faults to the fore and impose the most radical changes of all on the pattern of communications.

# 6 Modern Roads

Though the main national routes of Britain on the whole fell into decline with the coming of the railways, there was no real break in the development of roads. The demands of industry and commerce and, indeed, the traffic generated by the railways themselves, brought a steady increase in the use of roads, if over shorter distances than before. All roads became busier and the problem of their upkeep was forced more and more into the hands of government.

As early as 1835 the Highways Act, whereby Districts composed of groups of parishes with paid surveyors were set up, tried to find a way out of the difficulty. It was not a success, nor was the 1862 Highways Act which attempted to improve the earlier regulations, and even the 1878 Highways and Locomotive (Amendment) Act, under which properly constituted highway authorities were formed, failed to cope with the steadily increasing demands on the road system of the country. In 1889 the newly formed County Councils took over both responsibility for and the cost of main roads, and in 1894 the new Rural District Councils accepted responsibility for the local roads. But by then a revolution in road transport had begun: the advent of the internal combustion engine was to change the situation radically. The problem was twofold. One was the old spiral whereby an improvements result in the generation of more traffic, leading to further demands for improvement, a process which we have not properly appreciated even today. The other was the thoroughly British attitude of too little, too slow and too late. The increasing involvement of local authorities and central government was always forced on these organizations by outside events and thus no overall policy for transport was ever evolved. It was not until 1909 that central government made any grants to local authorities for roads, not until 1920 that a Ministry of Transport appeared, it was 1930 before the County Councils took over responsibility for all roads and

1936 before trunk roads became the financial responsibility of the Ministry of Transport.

As a result the history of roads in the last hundred years, far from being an example of modern efficiency and organization, has been merely the same as the previous 10,000 years but speeded up. It has been the piecemeal reaction to changing circumstances in individual locations. The great expansion of motor traffic in the 1920s and 30s is the prime example of this, for in those years individual loops of new road were wrapped around the unplanned expanding towns and villages with little thought for the future. These bypasses, together with the accompanying ribbon development along them, led eventually to the delights of the Kingston Bypass and North Circular Road. Only since the 1960s has any real transport policy in terms of national long-distance routes emerged, with the development of the motorway system. And even here we as a nation still have not come to grips with any final solution. The Americans saw the problem of continual self-generating traffic decades before Britain planned its motorways, but we failed to take note of it. Today we are terminating motorways on the edges of our urban areas, and wondering why they do not solve the problem. Or we cut swathes of hideous super-elevated concrete highways through our towns, to the total detriment of our environment, and still stand amazed at the continuing traffic jams.

In essence, of course, there is no answer to this problem. There are only two real alternatives – to go on building new roads until the whole country is a concrete desert and we are all prisoners in our own vehicles, or to rethink the whole of our social organization. The first solution is politically much easier, the second perhaps impossible to achieve in a democratic society. As a result the normal process of road development and the changes which have been catalogued in this book go on, only now much faster and much more destructively in terms of the social and visual environment. To take a simple example, when a new motorway is built with an interchange onto a trunk road which crosses it, even if it is in an apparently remote situation, it soon results in subsequent development which is even more horrifying than the motorway itself. Thus, on the M1 in Northamptonshire, at the Crick interchange where the Rugby to Northampton Road crosses it, a huge area has been built over by factories, warehouses and a motel. This, together with a considerable housing development at the village of Crick itself (Figs. 82, 83), relates to the focal point that the interchange creates. The planners with all their regulations find it hard to stop this kind of development. In Cambridgeshire, a planning department has been bombarded with applications for warehousing development around the site of a motorway junction which is still over two years away from completion. Most of these have been rightly rejected, but the pressures are enormous and cannot be completely ignored.

In less obvious but just as important ways, the changes in twentieth-century roads have altered much more than the roads themselves. Villages, farmsteads, hamlets and towns have all been changed by the availability of good roads. In rural areas, the decisions made in the 1920s and 30s as to which roads should be properly surfaced and which left as tracks have had enormous consequences in terms of social contact between communities and even in some cases the existence of communities themselves. Many small upland farmsteads and crofting communities in Scotland might well have survived if good roads to them had been constructed fifty years ago. Even in a county such as Northamptonshire the main reason why the, admittedly dying, village of Faxton was finally abandoned

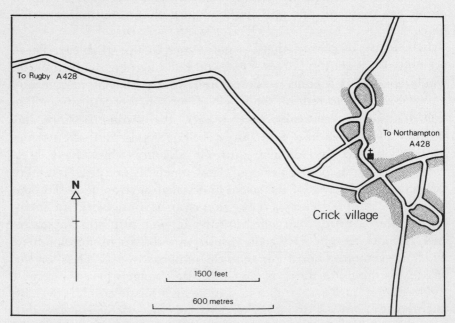

Fig. 82 Crick, Northamptonshire, 1957

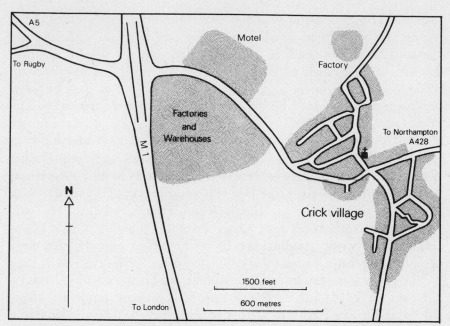

Fig. 83 Crick, Northamptonshire, 1977

at the end of the Second World War was the decision not to make up the roads leading to it. If the roads had been tarmaced, the village certainly would have survived and probably grown again with the recent demands for rural commuter housing.

Another example of a minor technological improvement for specific purposes having wider social implications can be seen in the fenlands of eastern England. There, up to the last war, most roads were unsurfaced droveways, impossible for traffic for weeks at a time, which had to be regularly ploughed to remove the ruts. The result was the existence of a community that tended to be isolated from both the outside world and its near neighbours. During the war, however, when the pressures to improve the productivity of the fens were considerable and when, in a war economy, finance was unlimited, the War Agricultural Committees laid down hundreds of miles of concrete tracks along the droveways to improve access to the land. These tracks not only succeeded in their immediate purpose, but later on completely changed the way of life of the fenland people to a degree which is hard to appreciate now, only thirty years later.

So roads go on being changed and with them our environment. Yet in spite of all that has happened we can, if we so wish, still see the total history of roads in our landscape. On the byroad north of Ancaster in Lincolnshire (Plate XV) we can drive on a narrow strip of tarmac set on top of a broad straight bank which runs between very wide verges, edged by dry-stone walls. We are here on the line of an ancient prehistoric track following the crest of the Lincoln Edge. The bank is the agger of the Roman Ermine Street between the towns of Ancaster and Lincoln. The wide verges are the product of the nineteenth-century enclosure surveyor who had to ensure that herds of cattle, moving to the towns of southern England as they had done for centuries, did not encroach upon the new fields. The narrow modern road is all that is necessary for what is now a minor route whose former importance has been taken over by the main Grantham to Lincoln road (A607) three miles to the east.

The prehistoric trackways, the Roman roads, the medieval tracks, the turnpike roads and all the rest are still with us. Some are abandoned and remain only to tell us of their past. Most are alive and allow us to live in the present.

# Gazetteer

The difficulty of dating and defining the period of use of roads and tracks has been one of the major themes of this book. Most trackways are in a sense ageless. This select list of some of the better known ancient tracks in Britain is intended in part to guide the traveller to the more interesting and visually attractive places. More important, however, it has been compiled to emphasize the point that all roads are the product of constantly changing circumstances which have altered them over the centuries.

## PREHISTORIC WAYS

### The Harroway

This route continues the Pilgrims' Way west from Guildford to Salisbury Plain. It shows well the different forms an ancient trackway can take today. The eastern part is now the main A31 trunk road between Guildford and Farnham. Beyond Farnham the Way is an almost continuous line of winding country roads and green lanes, except for a short section used by the A30 south of Basingstoke, as far as Andover where it becomes the main A303 to Amesbury and Stonehenge. None of it has any real appearance of antiquity but the most pleasant section runs between Whitchurch and Oakley, Hampshire (SU 466496–565509).

### The Icknield Way

This, perhaps the best known of all the ancient trackways of Britain, begins on the north coast of Norfolk, near Wells next the Sea. It runs via Swaffham, Newmarket, Royston and Luton to Goring, Oxfordshire, where it crosses the River Thames and becomes The Ridgeway. Most of it is followed by modern roads, for example the A11 and A505 between Newmarket and Baldock, or has been given the

characteristic straight alignments of the eighteenth- or nineteenth-
century enclosure surveyors. In places there appear to be multiple
trackways running generally north-east to south-west, all known as
the Icknield Way. Most of these are eighteenth or nineteenth century
in form and often have the familiar change of direction at parish
boundaries indicating their relatively modern origins and local purpose. An attractive route for walkers is along the green lane from
Streatley, north of Luton (TL 080265) to Ickleford, north of Hitchin
(TL 178313).

## The Jurassic Way

The traditional Jurassic Way is said to extend from Lincoln, via
Stamford, Northampton, Banbury, Stow-on-the-Wold and Bath to
Glastonbury. Except in a few places modern roads follow the line
and there are few visible signs of antiquity. One of the most interesting sections is the so-called Banbury Lane between Banbury and
Northampton. Whether it is more 'prehistoric' than any other road
in the area may be doubted, though it was certainly the main route
between these towns in medieval times. Part of its line is now the
modern A422 road and all the rest, apart from one short section, is
followed by existing roads. South of Moreton Pinkney (SP 580477–
610507) it remains an almost straight green lane. Even here, however, its form is largely the result of eighteenth-century alterations.

## The South Downs Ridgeway

This route is always said to begin somewhere near Beachy Head,
Sussex (TQ 595956) and to run along the northern edge of the South
Downs, crossing the River Cuckmere at Alfriston, the Ouse at
Lewes, the Adur at Steyning and the Arun at Houghton north of
Arundel, as far as the Iron Age hill fort of Old Winchester Hill,
south-west of Petersfield, Hampshire (SU 692206). There is indeed
an existing trackway along most of the route but the main reason for
its alleged antiquity is that it passes through areas rich in upstand-
ing prehistoric sites. Though modern destruction has removed most
of the evidence, old air photographs show that these downlands were
covered with tracks and roads of all periods, running in every direction. Thus while the Ridgeway may be prehistoric in origin it is only
part, and a very small part at that, of an immensely complex pattern
of communications, most of which is as old as the Ridgeway itself.

### The Pilgrims' Way (North Downs Ridgeway)

This ancient trackway extends from Canterbury, Kent, along the southern edge of the North Downs via Ashford, Maidstone, Caterham, and Dorking to Guildford, Surrey, where its continuation west is known as The Harroway. Its name derives from the fact that it was used by pilgrims in medieval times travelling to the shrine of St Thomas at Canterbury, though these pilgrims must have used many other routes as well. Presumably the same applies to pre-historic and Roman travellers, for there are many places where old holloways and tracks join and leave the main line. Long sections of the Pilgrims' Way are followed by modern roads where it has never fallen out of use. Among the best parts to walk are those at Albury Downs, east of Guildford (TQ 045493), between Wrotham and Halling south-west of Rochester (TQ 631609–688633) and on either side of the Mole gap north of Dorking (TQ 150506–187514).

### The Ridgeway

The name Ridgeway is commonly given to roads and tracks all over Britain, but the most famous is that through Berkshire. It continues the line of the Icknield Way from the crossing of the River Thames at Goring and runs along the northern edge of the Berkshire Downs to a point south of Swindon, Wiltshire. It then swings south along Hackpen Hill to just east of Avebury where it climbs onto Salisbury Plain. As with other ancient trackways it is lined with burial mounds, forts and other remains of prehistoric activity which give it a false importance. Less obvious because of modern agricultural destruction are the thousands of acres of prehistoric fields which, together with their trackways, lie on either side of it. When these are related to the Ridgeway it can be seen in its true light as one of many prehistoric routes across the landscape. By far the best part is that south of Wantage on the north side of the Lambourn Downs from Wanborough (SU 231814) via White Horse Hill and Chilton Downs to Streatley (SU 589815).

## ROMAN ROADS

### Ackling Dyke

This is the name given to the section of the Roman road from Salisbury to Dorchester where it crosses the Dorset Downs. To the south-east of Handley (SU 015164) the Roman road has not been used since the fifth century AD and remains as a massive bank or agger forty to fifty feet across and five to six feet high. It is one of the best surviving pieces of Roman road in Britain. A little further north on the present Salisbury to Dorchester road (A354), north-east of the hamlet of Woodyates (SU 033198) the road, again a large agger, dug into by medieval road repairers, can be seen. It lies north-east of Bokerley Dyke, a substantial bank and ditch which was built to block the Roman road in AD 367.

### Akeman Street (South)
Two Roman roads are known by this name. The most important is that which ran across the south Midlands from St Albans to Cirencester. Much of its eastern part is difficult to see but north-west of Tring the straight run of the main A41 to Aylesbury follows its alignment, as does part of the same road further north-west between Aylesbury and Bicester. Thereafter its line is not easily visible and in places is followed by only minor lanes. Nevertheless, many of the latter are well worth traversing, especially the section from just east of Cirencester to the north of Coln St Aldwyn, Gloucestershire (SP 065034–135054).

### Akeman Street (East)
This is the name given to the Roman road from Cambridge to Littleport, north of Ely, Cambridgeshire. The most well-marked section is that followed by the modern A10 from north-west of Waterbeach to the crossing of the Old West River (TL 482671–500716).

### Chute Causeway
This lies on the Roman road between Winchester and Mildenhall, Wiltshire, near the village of Chute (SU 3056). To avoid the steep valley of Hippenscombe and the high rounded chalk hill to the north, the Roman road turned in a broad arc to the west before regaining is original alignment. A modern lane lies on the Roman road but the nine short alignments which make up the diversion are still clearly visible.

### Dere Street
This is the Roman road from York leading to the River Forth in Scotland, probably built by Agricola in AD 79–80 as the main route for his drive to the north. Much of its length, south of the border, is

followed by modern roads, for it has always been an important route. However, between Bishop Auckland and Lanchester, Durham, near Binchester (NZ 204318), Hunwick (NZ 194326), Willington (NZ 192352) and Stockley (NZ 197380) is the series of bridges described in the text. North of Hadrian's Wall long sections of Dere Street are still well preserved across Northumberland and the Southern Uplands. Here are many fine examples of the work of Roman engineers in difficult terrain. There is a fine steep terraceway leading to the Sill Burn crossing, north of High Rochester, Northumberland (NY 824981), and on the north-east slopes of Woden Law, Roxburghshire, it appears as both a terraceway and a large agger up to thirty feet across (NT 794315).

### Devil's Causeway

The name suggests that the Dark Age people of Northumbria did not understand that this was the main Roman road which left Dere Street just north of Hadrian's Wall and ran for over fifty miles to Berwick upon Tweed. Much of it no longer exists and certainly most appears not to have been used after the end of the Roman period. What usually remains is a fine broad agger which can be seen in a number of places, for example at the crossing of the River Wansbeck, north of Hartburn (NZ 088866).

### Ermine Street

This was the main road from London to the north. The long straight length of Shoreditch High Street, Stoke Newington Road and Stamford Hill in north-east London is a good example of a Roman road, if not in the most attractive environment. Further north the Ermine Street shows well both its original form and later history. South of Royston, Hertfordshire (TL 355309–358395) it is a fine straight road, now followed by the modern A10. However, the deep cuttings and easy gradients reflect the improvements carried out on it since the late seventeenth century. North of Royston, though the modern road (A14) remains generally on the Roman road alignments, it has never had any major modern improvement and thus not only do the gradients on the hills remain steep, but the actual carriageway has been distorted over the centuries, producing many minor bends. From Alconbury Hill, Cambridgeshire, to a little north of Stilton (TL 186780–158917) the Ermine Street is now the A1. The present dual carriageway has obscured all trace of the original road though the straight, nine-mile long run is the Roman alignment. At Water Newton, Cambridgeshire, the A1 leaves the Ermine Street and the Roman road may still be seen as a huge bank crossing the site of the Roman town of Durobrivae (TL 122970) south of the River Nene and, on the north side of the river, crossing the fields south of Ailsworth (TL 113983). In Lincolnshire, north-east of Grantham, on either side of Ancaster (SK 984436) the Ermine Street, here known as High Dyke, is a minor road. Here the agger is still visible, running between wide verges left by the eighteenth- and nineteenth-century enclosure surveyors for the droving of cattle.

### Foss Way

Originally the frontier road marking the edge of the early Roman province, the Foss Way extends from Lincoln via Leicester, Cirencester, Bath and Ilchester to Axminster. Though most of it is still followed by modern roads and tracks there are long sections of green lanes with the remains of the original agger still visible. A good example is the long run between Grittleton, Wiltshire, and Rodmarton, Gloucestershire (ST 841796–965974). One of the most impressive parts of the Foss Way, still largely undisturbed, is that north-west of Newark, Nottinghamshire, where the original agger lies immediately west of the present A46 road to Lincoln (SK 825573). There it is a well-marked ridge thirty feet across and two feet high.

### Gartree Road

The section of the Roman road between Leicester and Stanion, near Corby, Northamptonshire, is traditionally known by this name. A fine piece of the original agger is preserved in Hazel Wood, on the south-east side of Corby (SP 872886), but the best part is the nine-mile long stretch of green lanes and byroads from near Glooston, Leicestershire, to the outskirts of Leicester (SP 743958–SK 630019).

### The Great Road

The name suggests that this, the Roman road from London to Colchester, was always important even after the Roman period. Its western part is now the main route through the outer suburbs of London via Forest Gate, but beyond Romford the old A12 follows the original line fairly closely. Apart from the long straight alignments, modern alterations have made it very different from its original form.

*King's Street*

This is the name given to the Roman road between the town of Durobrivae, west of Peterborough, and Bourne. It runs along the edge of the Lincolnshire fens and much of it is followed today by minor roads. One of these, from just south-west of Helpston, Cambridgeshire, to a little north-west of Baston, Lincolnshire (TF 113026–106137) is a fine eight-mile long straight alignment crossing the lower Welland Valley.

*Maiden Way*

This is a very isolated Roman road which ran across the Pennines from Kirby Thorpe, near Appleby, to the centre of Hadrian's Wall. The finest section is that across Melmerby Fell and Gilderdale Forest from Kirkland to a little to the north-west of Alston (NY 645325–695487). Here is a fine track with an agger, terraceways and the abutments of a bridge where it crossed Rowgill Burn (NY 673413).

*Pedars Way*

This is the Roman road running north-west across Norfolk from Coney Weston, Suffolk, to Holme next the Sea on the coast. It is one of the best Roman roads to walk along; for most of its length it is now followed by footpaths and green lanes and no main roads run along it. Fine walks are possible especially to the north and south of East Wretham (TL 934872–906967). Further to the north-west between Anmer and Fring the agger is especially well marked up to forty feet across and two feet high, running straight for over four miles (TL 754293–734343).

*The Port Way*

Many old roads are known as Port Ways, usually because in the Dark Ages or in medieval times they led to a 'port' or market town. The best known is the Roman road from Silchester, south of Reading, to Salisbury. Long sections of it were abandoned, probably in early Saxon times. This is especially true of the part near Silchester. Further south-west around Andover it remains in use and is marked by long straight stretches of country lane. The south-west part between Old Sarum and Winterbourne Gunner (SU 138327–178355) is another fine alignment.

*Ryknild Street*

This was one of the main Roman roads of the Midlands, running
from the Foss Way at Bourton-on-the-Water, Gloucester via Alcester
and Birmingham to cross the Watling Street at Wall, near Lichfield,
Staffordshire. It then turned north-east and ran to Derby and then
north to Templeborough, near Rotherham. The southern part across
the Cotswolds is only a green lane in some places and elsewhere
nothing but the abandoned agger survives. It is particularly well
worth walking along the section to the west of Stow-on-the-Wold
(SP 162248–152278). It descends the Cotswold scarp at Weston
Subedge and continues north-west as existing minor or main roads.
Its route through the Birmingham conurbation is not notable but
beyond Lichfield is a fine straight alignment crossing the Trent Valley as far as Burton upon Trent. This is now the main A38. The
same alignment continues beyond Burton to Derby making a total
length of over twenty miles. After Derby the line of Ryknild Street
is less well defined.

*Sarn Helen*

The main Roman road along the western side of Wales ran from
Carmarthen via Aberystwyth and Dolgelly to the Conway Valley.
Much of it is over difficult country and parts of it have not yet been
identified with certainty. It often shows interesting engineering
details resulting from the excessive slopes it traverses: for example,
on the A485 road south-east of Aberystwyth, immediately south of a
place called Lledrod (SN 642695), it is a terraceway running along
the steep hillside. However, perhaps the best section, unencumbered
by modern roads and with good evidence of terraceways, zig-zags
and cuttings, is that to the east of Blaenau-Ffestiniog (SH 738459–
717413) where it crosses Manod Mawr.

*Stane Street (South)*

This is the Roman road between London and Chichester and much
of it remains in use today. It is of special interest as its alignments
show the principles behind the laying out of Roman roads. The exact
line between London Bridge and Chichester was established and
actually followed by the road as far as Ewell, Surrey. The road was
then turned to pass through the Mole Gap at Dorking. The present
road (A3, A24) through south London, via Tooting and Merton,
follows the original alignment. Further south-west, beyond Dorking,

long runs of the A29 mark the original road as far as Pulborough, Sussex. Beyond the road has to climb the steep scarp of the South Downs and here it deviates slightly to make use of a convenient spur to the north of Bignor Hill (SU 983136). Across the summit of the escarpment the road remains as a massive agger, up to thirty feet wide, running across the downs towards Chichester (SU 970128–945110).

### Stane Street (East)

Another Stane Street is the Roman road from Braughing, Hertfordshire, to Colchester. It is followed, almost entirely, by the modern A120 road via Bishop's Stortford, Great Dunmow and Braintree. It is of considerable interest in that the road is made up of a number of relatively short alignments created to suit the rather broken terrain. This is especially notable around the village of Takeley where there are no less than six slight changes of alignment within four miles (TL 550212–605215).

### Stone Street

This fine Roman road, fifteen miles long from Canterbury to Lympne, Kent, includes a single ten-mile straight alignment. It is now followed by the B2068 road for much of its length. Particularly interesting is the point at which the road descends the scarp of the North Downs to the south of Stowting (TR 135404). Here it appears to turn in a broad curve to minimize the steep slope, but in fact the curve is made up of a series of short straight lengths.

### Wade's Causeway

The Roman road across the North York Moors from Malton to Whitby is known by this name. On Wheeldale Moor (SE 805975) a three-quarter mile length has been exposed and cleared by the Department of the Environment as a national monument. The road is surfaced with large stones, and traces of small culverts, put in by the engineers for drainage, are still visible.

### Watling Street

Perhaps the best known of the main Roman roads, the Watling Street ran from Canterbury to London and then across the Midlands to the north-west. Beyond London most of its line is followed by the modern A5. Apart from its characteristic straight alignments, often running for many miles, there is little that remains of its Roman date. Much of it has the mark of Telford's work of the 1820s when it was improved to form the Holyhead Road, hence the deep cuttings and finely graded inclines. Elsewhere more modern improvements have obscured even Telford's work. Among the more notable parts are the complex changes of alignment at the crossing of the River Nene at Weedon Bec, Northamptonshire (SP 632598), part of the original agger, abandoned in Saxon times near Kilsby, Northamptonshire (SP 570730), and the long fifteen-and-a-half mile alignment from Gailey, Staffordshire, to Wellington, Shropshire (SJ 910106–664110).

## Well Path

This name refers to the Roman road which ran across the Southern Uplands from Crawford, Lanarkshire, south-west into Nithsdale. Its north-eastern section is confused by the fact that the Roman road, an old medieval road and the modern A702 all run close together. Further south-west, however, the Roman road runs alone up the valley of the Potrail Water, though the pass between Well Hill and Durisdeer Hill and down the Kirk Burn to Durisdeer (NS 925084–895038). The present track there still shows traces of the original agger, causeways over marshy ground and terraced zig-zags down steep slopes.

## DARK AGE ROADS

### Herepaths

There are many tracks with this name. Probably the most famous and certainly one of the best to walk along is the Wiltshire Herepath, which extends across Fyfield and Overton Downs between Marlborough and Avebury (SU 175704–104701). Its name indicates that it was thought of as a track used by soldiers in the Saxon period. However, it could also be considered as a prehistoric trackway as it leads into the Avebury stone circle and it was certainly part of the Great West Road between London and Bath up until the eighteenth century. Indeed a field on Manton Down is still called 'London Road Ground'. On the higher parts of the downs it is a fine trackway with numerous traffic ruts and holloways cutting across one of the best-preserved areas of chalk grassland in southern England. On either side are the remains of prehistoric fields, some of which have later medieval ploughing over them. On Overton Down (SU 125708) the herepath is crossed by another track, The Ridgeway, on its way south to Salisbury Plain.

## Salt or Salters Roads

There are numerous salt or salters roads all over Britain which take their name from the commodity which was transported along them. Most are first recorded in the medieval period but must be much older. Those radiating from Droitwich, Worcestershire have been described in the main text. Others are centred on Nantwich, Cheshire. Among these are the Roman road running north-west via Northwich to Manchester, most of which is the present A556 and A56 road, the present A51 to Chester and the A534 to Wrexham. None has any visible signs of antiquity.

## Saxon Wegs or Ways

There are innumerable ways mentioned in Saxon or Dark Age documents, most of which can be identified on the ground. The most common are those recorded in charters which defined the boundaries of Saxon estates. Three examples may be given to indicate their appearance today. A charter of AD 994 for an area of land which includes the present parishes of Badby, Newnham and Dodford, in Northamptonshire, gives one point on the boundary as 'the holloway at the deer leap'. This can be exactly identified as a point on the present by-road between Daventry and Newnham where the latter slices through the hillside in a deep cutting (SP 576610). Another charter of 938 gives the boundaries of the parish of Uplyme, Devon. One major part of this boundary is a track called 'the Red Way'. It has been established that this is the existing A373 road between Charmouth, Dorset, and Axminster, Devon (SY 315963–342953). A third charter, of 943, defines the boundaries of an area of land near Whiteparish, Wiltshire. At one point the boundary meets 'the Hedged Way'. This too has been identified as the existing but little used track which runs across the chalk uplands from Witherington Down towards the village of Redlynch (SU 208243–204218).

## MEDIEVAL ROADS

### The Chester Road

This, the main medieval road from London to the north-west, used the Roman Watling Street (now the A5) as far as Weedon Bec, Northamptonshire. It then turned north-west and ran on to Coventry along what is now the main A45 via Daventry. Leaving Coventry along the line of the present A423 it crossed the Watling Street south of Tamworth, Staffordshire, passed through that town and entered Lichfield. It then went via Stone (A51), Newcastle under Lyme (A34) and Nantwich (A52) to Chester. There were in addition some alternative routes including the direct Stone to Nantwich road (A51) which bypasses Newcastle. There are few signs of antiquity along this road, though in some places, such as the deep cutting at Hopwas, between Tamworth and Lichfield (SK 170050), its long usage is obvious.

### The Exeter Road

This, the main route to the south-west, ran via Guildford, Winchester, Salisbury, Shaftesbury and Sherborne. The most interesting section is that between Salisbury and Shaftesbury. The present road (A30) runs via Wilton along the foot of the chalk downlands. The medieval road follows the ridgetop to the south, returning to the modern road down the steep slopes of Whitesheet Hill. A fine green lane, some thirteen miles long, follows the old road today (ST 933240–SU 134283).

### The Great North Road

This was a road with a number of alternative routes on its way from London to the north via York. The southern section is perhaps the most interesting. The older road is represented today by the A10 from London to Royston, Hertfordshire, and from Royston via Huntingdon to Alconbury Hill by the A14. Much of this followed the line of the Roman Ermine Street. This section is still called the Old North Road to distinguish it from the later Great North Road, the present A1, via Hatfield, Stevenage and Biggleswade to Alconbury Hill. This, though used in medieval times, was of lesser importance than the route via Royston. From Alconbury Hill, medieval travellers had a number of alternative routes, described in the main text of the book, as far as the crossing of the River Nene at Wansford, Cambridgeshire. The road then ran on along the line of the present A1 to Stamford, where, after crossing the River Welland, it rejoined the Ermine Street and ran on as far as Colsterworth, Lincolnshire. Along this section the straight Roman alignments are visible. At

Colsterworth the Great North Road turned and followed the lower ground west of the Ermine Street to Grantham and Newark, where the River Trent was crossed, and then took a very winding course through Tuxford, Nottinghamshire. Just to the south of Retford there were again alternative routes which included the present road through Retford via Bawtry to Doncaster and at least three others to the west via Blyth and Harworth which returned to the present Al at Barnby Moor, Bawtry or Rossington.

## The Great West Road

Until the construction of the M4 the main road to Bath and the west from London was the A4 via Slough, Reading, Marlborough and Chippenham. This was, at least in part, the medieval Great West Road. The first part of the medieval road from London used the old Roman road as far as Staines, hence the fine straight alignment of the A4 between Kew Bridge and Hounslow (TQ 135756–190781). At Hounslow the medieval travellers left the Roman road and turned west through Slough, crossing the River Thames at Maidenhead. They then passed through Reading and moved along the north side of the Kennet Valley to Hungerford. From this point two alternative routes were used. One continued along the River Kennet via Ramsbury and Mildenhall to Marlborough, the so-called Ramsbury Way. The other, now the A4, climbed up through Savernake Forest and then down back to the Kennet at Marlborough. The old holloways and ruts, made by medieval travellers using the second route, can still be seen for two miles on the south side of the A4 just south-east of Marlborough (SU 201688–233678). The present main road was finally established through the forest when this section was turnpiked in the mid eighteenth century. To the west of Marlborough there was a variety of routes. One, the present A4, ran on along the Kennet Valley, round the foot of Cherhill Down and so to Calne, Wiltshire. Another left Marlborough and threaded its way among the prehistoric fields on Overton and Fyfield Downs, following the Wiltshire Herepath to Avebury and thence back to the A4 at Beckhampton. Here was another choice of routes. Some travellers took one of two alternative tracks which still cross the higher slopes of Cherhill Down and then back to Calne. Others went south-west along the present A361 road towards Devizes, then swung off it and climbed over the downs to Lacock and so on to Bath. All these routes were also abandoned when the present A4 was turnpiked.

*The Norwich Road*

Today the main road from London to Norwich is the A11 which runs via Harlow, Bishop's Stortford, Newmarket, Thetford and Wymondham. In medieval times the route taken was rather different. The Great North Road was followed as far as Puckeridge in Hertfordshire. Then travellers had three alternatives. They could continue on to Royston and thence by the present A10 to Cambridge, where they turned east to Newmarket. Or they could turn off the Great North Road at Puckeridge and follow what is the modern B1368 via Barkway, Hertfordshire, and Fowlmere, Cambridgeshire, to Cambridge. They could also turn off the road near Fowlmere, and travel along the line of the Icknield Way, now the A505 and A11, to Newmarket, thus avoiding Cambridge.

Beyond Newmarket the road again divided to cross the River Lark. One route was the present A11 via Barton Mills, another left the A11 and went via Kennet, Cambridgeshire, Herringswell and Tuddenham, Suffolk, to cross the River Lark at Temple Bridge. The third route followed what is now the A45 towards Bury St Edmunds and then turned north-east to Cavenham where the tracks again divided, crossing the Lark at Icklingham or Lackford. All these routes then ran on across the Breckland where their lines can still be seen today as Six Tree Road (TL 766738–775768), Seven Tree Road (TL 769733–785779), Pilgrim's Path (TL 774776–806770) or the Icknield Way (TL 789712–846808). These tracks all converged again to cross the Little Ouse at Thetford and then separated again into at least three routes, the present A11, the minor road via Bridgham along the River Thet or north via East Wretham, before again converging at Attleborough.

*The Wheel Causeway*

This is the name given to a number of linked tracks and roads across the England-Scotland border. One of these was certainly the main road from Jedburgh to Carlisle in the thirteenth century. Most of the lines of its varied routes in Roxburghshire are away from modern roads and many of the details of an old upland trackway are visible. In places it is an apparently deliberately raised roadway (NY 602000), in others there are multiple tracks (NY 597992) and near Jedburgh itself it divides into at least three quite separate routes. However, though the Wheel Causeway was certainly used in medieval times, it is almost certainly much older. In addition, large sections were used by cattle drovers in the eighteenth and nineteenth centuries.

## POST-MEDIEVAL ROADS

By this period it is difficult to identify newly created roads by their individual names. A few of the most interesting ones are described below.

### Cadger's Loan

A number of Scottish trackways have this name as a result of their traditional use by cadgers or hawkers. One, between Stirling and Falkirk, was certainly used by pack horses in the eighteenth and nineteenth centuries, though no signs of antiquity are visible in the modern road.

### Drove Roads and Packhorse Trails

There are countless drove roads all over Britain and the best are the long-distance routes from Wales and Scotland to the Midlands and south of England used in the eighteenth and early nineteenth centuries. One of the more illuminating is that called The Welsh Road which runs across south-western Northamptonshire from Wormleighton in Warwickshire to Culworth in Northamptonshire. There it joins the Banbury Lane which is part of the alleged Jurassic Way. It is entirely a minor road today but at one point, north of Aston le Walls (SP 494511), an older line a little to the south-west can be traced. This is now a holloway which has been partly destroyed by a group of medieval fishponds. This indicates that the route is probably much older than its relatively recent use as a drove road would suggest.

A fine upland droveway is that which ran from Falkirk in Scotland via Peebles into the North Tyne Valley in Northumberland. For much of its southern part, across the Southern Uplands, it is still in its early nineteenth-century condition. Again all the features of this type of road are visible. The crossing of Eildon Quaw, in Roxburghshire (NT 354133), is on a dry stone culvert thirty feet across. This is far too wide for walkers or carts, but ideal for cattle. On the west side of Penchrise Pen (NT 487062) there is a main holloway edged by deeply worn subsidiary hollows, while tributary tracks joining the main one are visible on the east side of Hat Knowe (NT 806030).

*Military Roads*

These roads, dating from the first half of the eighteenth century, are common in Scotland where they were constructed after the 1715 and 1745 uprisings. Many are still used as modern roads, as is that across the Cairngorm Mountains from Balmoral to Tomintoul (A939). More interesting as a road is that along the south-eastern side of Loch Ness between Inverness and Fort Augustus (NH 662430–380090). Part is now the A862 but the northern half is followed by a minor road.

In more remote country, the A87 from Invermoriston to the Kyle of Lochalsh is mainly on the line of a military road along Glen Shiel. In places the older road runs parallel to the modern one and shows traces of its original causeways and culverts over streams (NH 060115–NG 998131).

# Index